aula Bethen

PRincepal /

Kilmea Schools

To learn more about educational resources
offered by the IIRP, please visit:
store.iirp.edu

Restorative Circles in Schools

A Practical Guide for Educators

by
Bob Costello
Joshua Wachtel
Ted Wachtel

INTERNATIONAL INSTITUTE FOR RESTORATIVE PRACTICES
Bethlehem, Pennsylvania, USA

INTERNATIONAL INSTITUTE FOR RESTORATIVE PRACTICES
531 Main Street
Bethlehem, PA 18018 USA

BOOK DESIGN
Alexis Van Saun

LIBRARY OF CONGRESS CONTROL NUMBER: 2019938881
ISBN-13: 978-193435544-2
ISBN-10: 193435544-5

LCCN: LB3013.3 .C68 2019
DDCN: 371.5 C841R 2019

Table of Contents

Note for Readers Outside the US

Administrator, Principal and Vice Principal

The term "administrator" refers to principals and vice principals (or assistant principals). The principal and vice principal are analogous to the head teacher and deputy head in the British system. Elementary schools generally have only a principal, while middle schools and high schools may have a principal and one or more vice principals or assistant principals (depending on the size of the school).

"Administrator" also refers to more senior-level positions responsible for the oversight of multiple schools in a school district — an administrative unit comprised of schools within a geographic area.

Disciplinarian

The term "disciplinarian" is sometimes a job title. Typically, however, responsibility for carrying out disciplinary measures in a school falls to a designated vice principal, or the principal where there is no vice principal.

Types of Schools, Grades and Ages

The following chart shows the types of schools and corresponding grades and ages. The split between elementary and middle school and between middle school and high school varies.

SCHOOL	GRADE	AGES
ELEMENTARY SCHOOL (PRIMARY)	KINDERGARTEN	5–6
	1	6–7
	2	7–8
	3	8–9
	4	9–10
	5	10–11
MIDDLE SCHOOL (SECONDARY)	6	11–12
(SOMETIMES "JUNIOR HIGH SCHOOL")	7	12–13
	8	13–14
HIGH SCHOOL (SECONDARY)	9 (FRESHMAN)	14–15
(SOMETIMES "SENIOR HIGH SCHOOL")	10 (SOPHOMORE)	15–16
	11 (JUNIOR)	16–17
	12 (SENIOR)	17–18

Note About the Second Edition

This edition includes several new anecdotes and minor changes to style. Thanks to IIRP Lecturer Mary Jo Hebling for her support and invaluable input.

CHAPTER 1

Two Stories

A restorative practices specialist was invited by a school to do a session with a fourth-grade class at an elementary school in Michigan. Bullying had become prevalent in the class, and a variety of attempts had been made to deal with the issue. The walls were covered with posters warning against bullying and why it shouldn't happen, students had written essays about the issue, and experts had been called in to give lectures about the dangers of bullying, but nothing had made a difference. No one had actually addressed the issue head-on with the active involvement of the children.

The restorative practices specialist came into the class and arranged the students in a circle. The teacher and principal of the school were also present. The specialist started the circle with an icebreaker, a simple go-around question that gave the children an opportunity to express something about themselves — an activity that didn't feel threatening. He asked, "What is something you like to do in your free time?" By answering the question the children began feeling comfortable talking to one another in the circle. Then the facilitator gave each child a colored ribbon and asked the students to answer the questions, "Who in your life has influenced you in a good way to help make you the good person you are today? What did they give you?" These questions were more personal but positive. The idea was to create a connection ceremony. Students talked about their grandparents or parents, a teacher, friend or coach, and said that person had given them qualities like courage, love and respect. After each student spoke, they tied a ribbon onto the growing string of colored ribbons, a symbol of connection, which the students later hung in the cafeteria.

After that go-around the restorative practices specialist felt confident enough to begin addressing the deeper problems plaguing the class, but still in a safe way. He asked, "How do kids treat each other in this classroom?" Answers were short but honest, as students spoke in turn, going around the circle: "Bad." "Some kids are mean." "There's name calling." "People don't respect each other."

The next question was "How do you personally feel affected by this behavior?" Students responded that they felt hurt, angry, sad and scared.

Finally, for the next round the specialist asked, "Who is strong enough and courageous enough to admit that they had a part in this?" By this time, some of the children were comfortable enough to begin to admit their part in the bullying.

The last question really hit home: "Who needs to say something to help make things right?" Now some of the students apologized for having bullied other children. A few children who hadn't bullied anyone apologized, too. They said they were sorry they hadn't stopped the bullying, that they'd watched it happen, or that they had fed into it by egging the bullies on or laughing about it. Some students cried, and emotions ran high.

The circle ended with all the students making a commitment to stop behaving in a bullying way. They also promised to do something to stop bullying when they saw others doing it, by confronting the bullies or telling a teacher when it was happening.

The circle itself was powerful, and in the ensuing days, it became clear that the children were keeping their commitments. Bullying in that class simply stopped. Encouraged by the result, the principal of the school implemented regular circles for every class. The facilitator reported that in one year, the school reduced its discipline referrals by 70 percent.

On the first day of class every year, a high school science teacher who teaches various ages, grade levels and specialties asks students to do a circle go-around. The question is always the same. Students are asked to say their names, something they notice about the teacher or the classroom and a hypothesis based on their observation.

The teacher encourages the students by telling them it doesn't matter whether their conclusions are right or wrong. A student might say, for example, "I see a periodic table. I guess that means we're doing chemistry this year." As they go around, the teacher learns a little something about everyone, and the students begin to learn about each other, too. In addition, a basic scientific principle — the difference between observation and conclusion — has been introduced.

In one class a student said, "My name's Blake. I notice that your tie is very thin. So I'm guessing you haven't been clothes shopping in a while."

In this case, in less than ten minutes at the start of the year, the teacher had identified the class clown. The lesson came two months later during an experiment, when Blake dumped two test tubes into a beaker, and the beaker overflowed with bubbles. The class clown responded sarcastically, "Oh, look! A chemical reaction." The teacher replied, "No, it's a bunch of bubbles. That's all you have *observed*. But you have *concluded* that there's a chemical reaction, just like that conclusion you made about my tie the first day of school."

These two stories illustrate the wide range of ways that circles can be used in schools. The first demonstrates the power of a circle in dealing with behavior problems. The second shows its potential for academic purposes.

These days, with increasing pressure on teachers to show results on standardized tests, many teachers say they don't have time for more responsibilities. They feel that every new program instituted by a school cuts into educational time. This book makes the argument that fewer discipline referrals and better relationships within the classroom make for a better, more productive learning environment. The judicious use of circles provides *more* time for teaching and learning, not less.

The first story illustrates the powerful effect a restorative circle can have in a school when other efforts have failed. Teachers and administrators had talked about bullying, posted signs and brought in speakers, but none of this had a direct impact on the bullying. The seemingly simple act of actively engaging the children in a heartfelt discussion about the issue did have an impact — a powerful and lasting one.

But while the circle's potential for confronting bullying and other increasingly inappropriate behaviors attracts a great deal of attention, the proactive use of circles offers even greater promise for improving relationships, creating community and transforming the whole school environment. The second story is a funny example of one-upmanship, but it also demonstrates that circles can serve multiple functions. Teachers who use circles on a day-to-day basis advance curricular goals and build "social capital" at the same time.

CHAPTER 2

Restorative Practices

Circles, Restorative Justice and the IIRP

The circle is a potent symbol. Its shape implies community, connection, inclusion, fairness, equality and wholeness. Seating students in the rows of the traditional classroom, where they only see the teacher and some of their classmates' backs, limits connection and conversation. This arrangement is appropriate for lecture and other didactic modalities but does not lend itself to discussion. Meeting in a circle, with neither head nor tail, establishes a level playing field for all participants.

The use of circles for meeting and discussing issues has evolved in almost every culture. The first human circles resulted from the natural formation of people sitting around a fire, providing the best way to efficiently distribute access to heat and light. Many indigenous cultures maintain these traditions to this day. When schools and other groups arrange people in a circle, there is no fire but instead an issue or topic that is relevant to everyone gathered around. The circle for the fourth-grade class plagued with bullying held the promise of a kinder, more respectful and caring way for the students to behave toward one another.

In this book we present circles within the context of *restorative practices*, an emerging field of study that offers a common thread to tie together theory, research and practice in seemingly disparate fields, such as education, counseling, criminal justice, social work and organizational management.

The restorative practices concept has its roots in *restorative justice*, a way of looking at criminal justice that focuses on repairing the harm done to people and relationships rather than on punishing offenders (although restorative justice does not preclude incarceration of offenders or other sanctions). Originating in the 1970s as mediation between victims and offenders, by the 1990s restorative justice broadened to include communities of care, with victims' and offenders' families and friends participating in collaborative processes called "conferences" and "circles."

The International Institute for Restorative Practices (IIRP), a graduate school based in Bethlehem, Pennsylvania, envisions a comprehensive framework for practice and theory that expands the restorative paradigm beyond its origins in criminal justice. It offers master's degrees and graduate certificates in restorative practices. The IIRP also offers continuing education, produces videos and books (like this one) and organizes international conferences in the field of restorative practices.

The IIRP's demonstration schools and residential programs, Community Service Foundation and Buxmont Academy, were founded in 1977, and their history parallels the development of the restorative practices movement. In the late 1970s, CSF Buxmont, now a series of schools and foster group homes for delinquent and at-risk youth in eastern Pennsylvania, began experimenting with the use of circles in its first school. Counselors used circles to bring students together in its school/day-treatment counseling program to discuss problems, give each other feedback and take responsibility for establishing norms and rules and for enforcing those rules. Circles empowered troubled youth and helped them transform their own lives.

Similarly, in the 1980s the New Zealand family court system spearheaded a process called "family group conferencing," which brought families and close community members together to deal with a young person's misbehavior. Conference participants, seated in a circle, developed their own plans to help a child and family for whom they were concerned, in lieu of the family court imposing decisions from outside.

That process was subsequently borrowed and adapted by Terry O'Connell, an Australian police officer, to deal with youth crime. Provided with a scripted series of questions to foster discussion — a process that the IIRP named Real Justice® — the facilitator brings the offending youth and their families together with victims, as well as families and friends of the two parties. In the facilitated conference, conducted in the form of a circle, offenders who have admitted to their crimes are invited to explain what they have done, whom they think they have affected and what they see as the consequences of their misbehavior. Victims then have a chance to explain how they have been affected by the offender's misdeeds and how they feel about it. The supporters of both parties then have their say as well. Finally, the conference poses the question of how the harm might be redressed and agreements are drawn up.[1]

The IIRP grew out of these efforts in the late 1990s to bring Real Justice to North America and to train schools in the use of restorative practices through the SaferSanerSchools™ program (see http://www.iirp.edu/safersanerschools). While Real Justice responds to harm and wrongdoing, restorative practices include the proactive, preventative use of restorative approaches.

Social Discipline Window

A basic premise of restorative practices is that people (students, teachers and staff) are happier and more likely to make positive changes when those in authority (teachers, staff and

---

1. See *Restorative Justice Conferencing: Real Justice and the Conferencing Handbook* by Ted Wachtel, Terry O'Connell and Ben Wachtel, for practical details about the script and the process, the story of Ted Wachtel's personal journey into the field of restorative justice and examples of real cases resolved using restorative justice.

administrators) do things *with* them, rather than *to* them or *for* them.

The Social Discipline Window is a graphic that illustrates this premise and shows how restorative practices differs from other modes of discipline (see Figure 1).

THE SOCIAL DISCIPLINE WINDOW
Figure 1

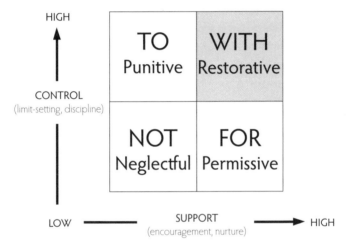

Adapted by Paul McCold and Ted Wachtel

The window is composed of two axes: support and control. Traditionally, these concepts are thought to be contradictory: that an authority only has the choice to be controlling and paternalistic or else nurturing and maternalistic. In actuality, though, a third option shows how both of these useful and necessary approaches may work together.

If support is graphed on an axis in one direction, from low to high, and control is graphed on the other axis, four quadrants representing four general possibilities for social discipline emerge. The top left, showing high control and low support, represents the authoritarian or punitive approach: doing things *to* people. This approach sets rules and holds people to them, with little need for explanation. Taken to its extreme, this approach is cold and distant: authoritarian.

The bottom right square — low control and high support — highlights the permissive approach. This attitude assumes that with nurturing alone people will make positive changes, but it often leads to protectiveness and doing things *for* people. It provides no mechanism for stepping in to set clear boundaries.

The bottom left, low support and low control, represents *not* doing anything. This is a neglectful stance, and it is destructive.

The area to the top right, where both control and support are high, is the corner we wish to highlight. This represents the positive synthesis of the best aspects of the punitive and permissive approaches. The restorative approach has been called "authoritative:" doing things *with* people. It combines high levels of control for setting boundaries and expectations with high levels of support and nurturing for people to succeed and make positive changes.

The Restorative Questions

Derived from the Real Justice conference, the restorative questions clarify the difference between restorative and other approaches to discipline. These questions can be placed on two lists: one for responding when things go wrong, the other for helping those who have been affected. Where two parties have mutually hurt one another, both lists of questions may be drawn from interchangeably.

The basic questions for responding when something goes wrong:
> What happened?
> What were you thinking about at the time?
> What have you thought about since?

> Who has been affected by what you have done? In what way?
> What do you think you need to do to make things right?

The basic questions for helping someone who has been affected by actions:

> What did you think when you realized what had happened?
> What impact has this had on you and others?
> What has been the hardest thing for you?
> What do you think needs to happen to make things right?

These questions seek to elicit the story of the actions and events, the thoughts and feelings associated with those actions and events and solutions for making things right, rather than assigning blame and seeking justifications for behavior. The questions create a feedback loop, so that people can hear how their actions have affected others, and encourage them to take responsibility for those actions. They also pave the way for solutions to problems to be found.

These questions help a person in authority walk the line between holding people accountable for their actions by addressing and not ignoring what has happened, and nurturing and supporting people by giving them useful questions to help them take responsibility for and resolve problems themselves. The outcome of an exchange using restorative questions tends to be restorative — that is, it tends to resolve the underlying issue and ease people's bad feelings.

These questions separate people's behavior from their intrinsic worth as a person, allowing them to admit their mistakes, right their wrongs and reintegrate into a community. "Separating the deed from the doer" prevents people from being stigmatized as "bad" and gives them an opportunity to change. The questions also allow a person in authority to place more responsibility for righting wrongs on those responsible for what has happened, rather than being in the position of judging, scolding and meting out punishment.

Note that the question "Why did you do that?" is not included in the list of restorative questions. Although "Why?" is often the first question asked by an authority dealing with an incident of wrongdoing, it tends to put people on the defensive and frequently results in no answer or a useless rationalization. People may not really know why they do things without a lot of self-reflection and will carelessly answer, "I don't know." In truth, inappropriate behavior is usually impulsive and thoughtless, so there really is no reasonable explanation.

Restorative questions tend to be non-blaming and open-ended, rather than loaded and leading. Restorative questions promote introspection, and they are as much for the benefit of the person being asked the questions as they are for the benefit of the questioner.

Many questions besides the ones listed above may also be considered restorative. In fact, according to one restorative practices expert, the listed questions are the default questions he uses when the situation very clearly involves a victim and an offender, or if he isn't quite sure what else to ask in a given situation. Many great restorative questions are not scripted but arise naturally.

In the opening story of this book, the circle facilitator said to the class after a number of go-arounds, "Now who's brave enough to admit they're part of the bullying problem?" If this question had been asked first it probably would have put the students on the defensive. But because the facilitator had built trust, at the moment he asked it the question was restorative.

Look at the implications behind the questions you ask students and the tone with which you ask them. If you bring the restorative philosophy to your practice, the questions you ask will build and restore relationships. Examples of other restorative questions will be found throughout this book. But, in the meantime, our standard restorative questions provide a ready template.

Restorative Practices Continuum

The Restorative Practices Continuum (see Figure 2) demonstrates that a range of actions by an authority may be restorative — from the formal conference and circles shown on the right of the continuum, to the less formal, daily use of affective statements and questions shown on the left. As you move from the informal to the formal, the restorative practices involve more people, more planning and more time. Formal processes, however, tend to be more complete and structured than informal ones and therefore more impactful.

THE RESTORATIVE PRACTICES CONTINUUM
Figure 2

INFORMAL				FORMAL
affective statements	affective questions	small impromptu conversations	circle	formal conference

Moving from the informal to the formal, the processes on the continuum are as follows:

The most informal process on the continuum is *affective statements*, which are simply expressions of personal feelings. Instead of scolding a student for breaking a rule, a teacher might identify the behavior and express how it makes them feel: "When everyone's talking at once and I'm trying to give directions, I feel very angry and frustrated with you." Affective statements help clarify boundaries, provide feedback and build empathy.

The restorative questions discussed above may also be called *affective questions*, because they get people talking about their feelings with one another. When a teacher witnesses a problem, like students arguing on the playground, affective questions can be used to address what has happened. "How do you think Suzie felt when you did that to her?" The questions give students a chance to tell their story and express their feelings about what has happened.

Small impromptu conversations occur when a few people meet briefly to address and resolve a problem. Modeled on more formal circles and conferences, a small impromptu conversation employs affective questions to facilitate a short interaction. If, for example, a few students in the back of a class are being disruptive, the teacher might approach them, ask what is happening, how they think their behavior might be affecting their classmates and what they need to do to change their behavior or make amends. This may only take a few minutes, and it allows students to help prevent the same thing from happening again.

Circles are a more formal restorative process. Examples of circles have been given in the first chapter, and many more will be discussed throughout this book. A class, a group of students or a group of adults meet in a circle to discuss, answer questions, solve problems, play a game or offer feedback. A circle has structure, purpose and focus. It may be proactive or responsive. The topic may be personal, academic or work related. Circles may be the most adaptable form of restorative practices on the continuum.

Finally, *formal restorative conferences* provide the most structure and require the greatest amount of planning. They are often reserved for dealing with serious problems of behavior when everything else has failed. Restorative conferences generally deal with criminal behavior but have been adapted for use in schools with students who have broken school rules. The Real Justice conference model described earlier in this chapter is one example of this type of conference.

Family group decision making (FGDM), also known as family group conferencing (FGC), engages families in a process of finding solutions for caring for a family member. The New Zealand model, mentioned earlier, is one example of this process. Schools have adapted this process for engaging families to work on issues such as poor academic performance, truancy, social phobias and bullying.

Fair Process

A primary goal of restorative practices is to foster participatory and cooperative community. When authorities do things *with* people, rather than *to* them or *for* them, the results almost always tend to be better. This idea was dubbed "fair process" in an influential article that appeared in *Harvard Business Review* (Kim & Mauborgne, January, 2013). Three components of fair process are:

> *Engagement* — involving individuals in decisions that affect them by listening to their views and genuinely taking their opinions into account;

> *Explanation* — explaining the reasoning behind a decision to everyone who has been involved or who is affected by it;

> *Expectation clarity* — making sure that everyone clearly understands a decision and what is expected of them in the future.

The first of two stories illustrates how fair process can work with students:

As the end of the year approached, a special-education teacher found herself in a familiar position. Standardized tests were coming up, and the teacher knew she needed to start prepping her students for these exams. But she still had a story to cover in class, along with an exam, both of which were required components of the curriculum. The teacher knew it would take two weeks to cover the story, but she had only one week left for preparation for the test. She felt stuck and didn't know what to do.

Invoking fair process, she decided to put the students in a circle and simply explain the problem. She admitted to the students that she didn't know what to do, and she asked them, "Do you have any ideas about how we can get everything accomplished?"

At first the students were taken aback that the teacher

would share all this information with them. But they sympathized with her and felt empowered by the way she enlisted their support. They immediately started thinking up ideas for how to solve the problem, and in a short time they developed a very creative plan. The class decided to split the story into its salient parts and assign two or three students to deal with each piece. Each group would compose and enact a skit to explain their part of the story to the rest of the class. They also developed a plan for ensuring that everyone followed through with their part of the task.

At the end of the week a day was set aside for skits, and everyone did a fantastic job. When the teacher gave the students the test, everyone finished it in one day, most scored higher than usual, and a number of them got 100 percent correct, which hardly ever happened in that class. The following Monday they were back on track for standardized test preparation. The teacher also reported that not only was the class fully engaged in their work during the story project, but they also had a great feeling of pride and a positive attitude toward the class that continued until the end of the year.

In the second story, fair process is demonstrated with school staff:

A school district was in the midst of contentious contract negotiations. Staff, administration, school board members and taxpayers in the community were all at odds. The press had been used to sling mud every which way and fan the flames. A strike seemed likely.

This acrimonious atmosphere cast a dark, bitter cloud over the first day of classes. Teachers in one school had an hour-long meeting before the students arrived, and the principal of the school decided to address the problem with a circle go-around. Teachers were asked to answer two questions:

1. What is one thing you know to be true about this school that you hope will not change?
2. What is one thing you are going to do to help ensure that those things do not change?

By placing the emphasis on the purposes of the school and common values rather than differences and political issues, a positive tone was established for the beginning of the school year and no problems were reported.

Fair process acknowledges that some people will always disagree with certain decisions. However, when people are truly engaged in a decision-making process, know their opinions have been heard and feel a sense of fairness has been applied, then they are more likely to go along with changes and new policies. This is true even when they disagree or would do things differently if they were in charge. The very act of genuinely listening to what people have to say changes the atmosphere and the dynamics in any situation.

Psychology of Affect

The most critical function of restorative practices is restoring and building relationships. Because informal and formal restorative processes foster the expression of affect or emotion, they also foster emotional bonds. The late Silvan S. Tomkins' writings about the psychology of affect (Tomkins, 1962, 1963, 1991) assert that human relationships are best and healthiest when there is free expression of affect — or emotion — minimizing the negative and maximizing the positive, but allowing for free expression. The late Donald Nathanson, founder of the Silvan S. Tomkins Institute, added that it is through the mutual exchange of expressed affect that we build community, creating the emotional bonds that tie us all together (Nathanson, 1995). Restorative processes such as conferences and circles provide a safe environment for people to express and exchange intense emotion.

THE NINE AFFECTS
Figure 3

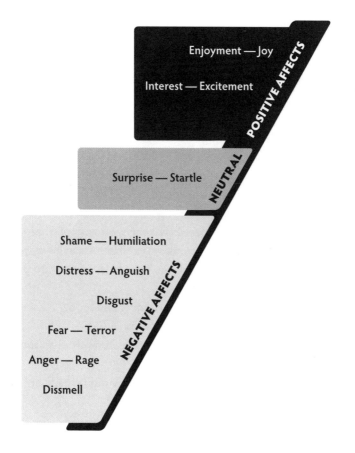

ADAPTED FROM TOMKINS, 1962, 1963 & 1991

Tomkins identified nine distinct affects (see Figure 3) to explain the expression of emotion in all human beings. Most of the affects are defined by pairs of words that represent the least and the most intense expression of a particular affect. The six negative affects include anger-rage, fear-terror, distress-anguish, disgust, dissmell (a word Tomkins coined to describe "turning up one's nose" at someone or something in a rejecting way) and shame-humiliation. Surprise-startle is the neutral affect, which functions like a reset button. The two positive affects are interest-excitement and enjoyment-joy.

Shame is worthy of special attention. Nathanson explains that shame is a critical regulator of human social behavior. Tomkins defined shame as occurring any time that our experience of the positive affects is interrupted (Tomkins, 1963). An individual does not have to do something wrong to feel shame. The individual just has to experience something that interrupts interest-excitement or enjoyment-joy (Nathanson, 1997). This understanding of shame provides a critical explanation for why victims of crime often feel a strong sense of shame, even though the offender committed the "shameful" act.

Nathanson (1992) has developed the Compass of Shame (see Figure 4) to illustrate the various ways that human beings react when they feel shame. These are the four poles of the compass of shame and their associated behaviors.

> *Withdrawal* — isolating oneself, running and hiding
> *Attack self* — self put-down, masochism
> *Avoidance* — denial, abusing drugs, distraction through thrill seeking
> *Attack others* — turning the tables, lashing out verbally or physically, blaming others

Nathanson says that the "attack others" response to shame is responsible for the proliferation of violence in modern life. Usually people who have adequate self-esteem readily move beyond their feelings of shame. Nonetheless we all react to shame, in varying degrees, in the ways described by the compass. Restorative practices, by its very nature, provides an opportunity for us to express our shame, along with other emotions, and in doing so reduce their intensity. In restorative conferences, for example, people routinely move from negative affects through the neutral affect to positive affects.

THE COMPASS OF SHAME
Figure 4

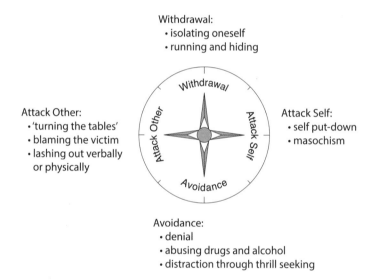

Withdrawal:
• isolating oneself
• running and hiding

Attack Other:
• 'turning the tables'
• blaming the victim
• lashing out verbally or physically

Attack Self:
• self put-down
• masochism

Avoidance:
• denial
• abusing drugs and alcohol
• distraction through thrill seeking

ADAPTED FROM NATHANSON, 1992

A Note About Ritual

Because circles have developed in a lot of different places and cultures, they have evolved with certain protocols, rituals and symbols, all of which are important to the specific cultures conducting those particular types of circles. The restorative practices specialist who incorporated a connection ritual using colored ribbons in the fourth-grade class plagued with bullying noted, "Many people are reluctant to do ceremonial things, but it can be emotional and transformative. A ritual says, 'We're taking time to do something different. We've been doing something a certain way, and we can take this moment to turn and take things in a new direction.' "

Kay Pranis, Barry Stuart and Mark Wedge, in their book *Peacemaking Circles: From Crime to Community*, describe the philosophy and practice of circles, paying special attention to Native American rituals associated with circles.

In this book, we will largely talk about the fundamental elements of circles without reference to the specific rituals associated with different cultures. Naturally, if one is conducting a circle for a group in a Christian church, starting the circle with a Christian prayer may not only be appropriate but important and necessary. Likewise, a Native American circle may begin with an invocation of a traditional song or chant, and a relevant symbol like an eagle feather may be used as a talking piece — the object that is passed around the circle to designate whose turn it is to speak.

Specific symbols and rituals can enhance the experience of the circle for the people involved, and many people's understanding of circles and their use is informed by the contexts in which they have experienced circles. But in an effort to make this book universally helpful, we will intentionally ignore many of the ritual aspects of the circle. This is not because we reject those ideas or fail to recognize their power, but because we want to present essential ideas about circles for an international readership, which will adapt circles to their own traditions.

CHAPTER 3

Proactive Circles

As schools and youth-serving organizations in urban, suburban and rural areas face increasing behavioral problems, interest in restorative practices in general and in circles specifically has grown. Restorative practices help deal with misbehavior, as well as the most serious problems, including violence, bullying and crime. Traditional punitive discipline does not achieve positive changes in student behavior and fails to address the breakdown of basic decorum. Using proactive circles before problems even occur, however, will begin the process of improving school climate and achieving the kind of durable solutions that schools need.

Why Circles?

A special-education teacher explains how circles help with classroom management by building positive relationships between students:

> I find that the more respect and knowledge the students have for one another, the smoother and better functioning my class becomes. In one class I have students who are part-time mixed with students who are full-time special-education students. With this rather large and diverse

group I find that a circle and group work helps unite this class.

A lesson that has gone well with this particular class uses the restorative circle and involves reading the local newspaper together. Each student has a newspaper, and after reading an article of his or her choosing (silently or out loud, depending on their reading level), each student "reports out" on the article. The other students are required to listen and not interrupt. When the "reporter" is finished, they will ask if anyone has any questions. The reporter is the facilitator of this activity. As the teacher, I rarely have to shut down a conversation, because each student generally wants their turn to "report out." However, I do use a timer if it is needed, allotting a specific amount of time for the task, so each student feels the activity has been fair. During this activity I also use an object [talking piece] to show which student has the floor. I have dragons, dinosaurs, cars and various other things to use.

My students are quite comfortable with each other at this time, and there is very little shyness with the "reporting out." Most of the students in my classes take reading class throughout high school, so I might be teaching the same kids for three years. I need for my students to show me what they know. My students also like being able to show their classmates what they know. This is a strategy that seems to work all the way around.

Circles, by their very structure, convey certain important ideas and values without the need for discussion:
> *Equality* — Everyone in the circle has equal seating.
> *Safety and trust* — You can see everyone in a circle, so nothing is hidden.
> *Responsibility* — Everyone has a chance to play a role in the outcome of the circle.

> *Facilitation* — The circle reminds the leader to facilitate rather than lecture.
> *Ownership* — Collectively, the participants feel the circle is theirs.
> *Connections* — These are built as everyone listens to everyone else's responses.

In the circle everyone can look one another in the eye. Students get equal time and attention, and they learn to trust each other and feel safe.

Because students cannot hide in the circle, everyone must participate. There are a remarkable number of students in schools who make it through entire school days without speaking at all in class. These students fly completely under the radar. Circles ensure that everyone is more engaged and that students can't hide out all day long.

When students don't know what to say in response to a circle question, teachers encourage them to enlist fellow students to help them think of answers, which further builds connections and a mutually supportive atmosphere.

Eventually, students begin to help facilitate their own circles, which builds confidence and a sense of responsibility. They take risks, both academically and personally, and talk about feelings, ideas, what they read, themselves and others. Students both give and listen to feedback.

In circles, students, teachers, disciplinarians, administration, staff and parents express themselves in ways they rarely do otherwise. The perspectives, facts and stories shared in the circle cultivate empathy and influence behavior.

Using circles first and foremost to establish strong, supportive relationships among students has a significant academic impact in the long run. Some teachers fear they are being asked to become therapists, because they know that circles have been used in therapeutic settings and because circles are a forum for the free expression of affect. But as great teachers know, teaching is much more than conveying facts and information alone. There is a significant interpersonal dimension to teaching.

A basic premise of restorative practices is that the increasingly inappropriate behavior in schools is a direct consequence of the overall loss of connectedness in our society. By fostering inclusion, community, accountability, responsibility, support, nurturing and cooperation, circles restore these qualities to a community or classroom and facilitate the development of character. As a consequence of fostering relationships and a sense of belonging, academic performance also flourishes.

Getting Started with Circles

When using circles proactively, there is a need to balance two factors: helping students get to know each other better and delivering course content. To the first end, icebreaker questions like "How was your weekend?" or "Where would you go if you had the resources to go anywhere?" are useful. At the same time, circles can be used to deliver and process course content. Relevant circle questions and activities can be designed and structured for any course.

The idea of running circles, when they are new and unfamiliar, can trigger fear and resistance in children and adults. The trick is to get over the initial hurdle. Introduce circles when things are going well. Design an activity to familiarize students with the idea of circles, build the confidence of the facilitator and the participants and enhance relationships.

This testimonial from a high school business teacher illustrates how he overcame his own initial jitters about using circles and how, through the natural development of a circle discussion, a single circle met the dual needs of getting students to know each other and advancing the curricular agenda:

As a new teacher the thought of using a "circle" seemed both intriguing and intimidating. Our building principal not only voiced his support of the program, but also cleared the way for all new teachers to receive training in the use of restorative practices.

After the three-day training session and with guidance from our principal, it was made clear that the "circle" was to be used as a learning instrument and not just a touchy-feely, get-to-know-you time filler. I made the commitment to use the methods learned in as many venues as possible. Being new, I thought, "It doesn't hurt to see what works." Furthermore, I was told that most students at the high school were versed in the process and actually enjoyed its use in class. I was pleased to find this was the case.

Personally, restorative practices has become a great tool, for not only increasing student ownership in the class-room, but also for effectively administering curriculum. Students instinctively "circle up" and follow the rules. I have used the circle to give direct instruction, summarize lessons, solicit student feedback and discuss various topics. By its nature, the circle allows each student to be part of the group and have direct input. No one hides in the circle.

Recently, I used the circle to discuss consumer credit rights in my Personal Finance class. I began with the standard probe question and led the group in the direction I had hoped to go. Most students had given an answer as to their interpretation of the rights of credit card users. As we made our way around the circle, I could see the concern on several students' faces as they processed the information. Within a few seconds hands began to go up requesting another chance to speak. The patience of two students was wearing thin. They needed to know.

Being savvy users of the circle, one of them "piggy-backed" another student's answer by offering some input and posing a question to the student. She was soliciting feedback with a question of her own. Immediately after the question was asked, two additional students looked at each other and nodded as if to say, "That's what I want to know!" Without my help, our circle had taken on a very personal tone. Not only was the material being processed, but students were using the circle to find answers. The overriding concern of the students was the difficulty their parents were experiencing from overuse of credit cards, and students earnestly wanted to know what rights and remedies were available to help.

That circle led to one of the most interactive and thoughtful classes I've experienced. Students knew the purpose. They knew the rules. And ultimately, they knew how to experience positive personal growth through the process. All I did was lead the horse to the water, and the horse took a big gulp.

When a teacher conducts their first circle, they may be nervous. Students unfamiliar with the circle process may also find it intimidating. When you start with something that feels safe and is not too difficult, you increase the chances of having a successful experience.

Whatever topic you choose, be sure to present clear guidelines and goals for the circles. Explain what circles are about; they are a way for students to get to know one another and a chance for people to support each other personally and academically. Explain that people are expected to participate and take the circle seriously. People must not tease or laugh at one another. The circle is a place where people need to feel safe to share their ideas. If someone doesn't know what to say, they may ask for suggestions.

Also articulate the purpose of the specific circle. "What is one of your favorite [fill in the blank]?" is a good icebreaker question. (This is preferable to "My favorite ..." because sometimes people take this too literally and get stymied thinking of their *absolute* favorite, whereas coming up with "*one* of my favorite things" is often easier to answer.) Other possibilities include asking students to talk about hobbies, interests and goals. They may also talk about a quality that makes a person a good friend or a good student. A simple feelings check can be a quick and easy icebreaker, too. The answer may be a word or a short sentence.

If you want to make your circle more appropriate to the academic subject at hand, think in terms of what is being taught in your class. In a geography class the question may be, "Where is the farthest place you've traveled or one of your favorite places?" In an English class, "What is one of your favorite books or authors?" In science, "Have you ever done an experiment? What was it?" In physical education, "How often do you exercise, or what sports and physical games do you like to play?" Many of these things are questions teachers already ask students to answer in written form or with a partner. It is easy to transfer these ideas to the circle format:

A math teacher wondered how he could ever do content circles in math class. Then it dawned on him that he could use a circle to share "exit ticket" content, an activity that students had to complete before they left class each day. On the exit ticket, students recorded what they had learned, along with their struggles and needs from the teacher.

During a weekly circle, the teacher invited students to share what they had written on their tickets. The teacher found that he was able to assess how the students were learning much more quickly. Students began to connect with other students who shared their strengths and weaknesses in math. Once the routine was established, the teacher also began to add fun community-building go-arounds.

A sentence starter, especially for younger students, can be a big help: "I like it when my friend ..." "The best thing about today was

..." "My best memory from the last year was when ..." In a language class, this type of sentence starter can also be used to teach proper use of newly learned sentence structures.

As you get to know your students and they get to know one another, questions may become more personal or more challenging. But it is important to make students comfortable with the circle process first.

A principal at a charter school introduced the concept of circles to her staff with the question, "Talk about something embarrassing that has happened to you." People felt uncomfortable and some blurted out outrageous things they wouldn't normally talk about with acquaintances they did not know well. She learned the hard way that you need to begin with something safe and easy and let people gain confidence by sharing more personal information by degrees.

This is one of the good reasons to try to make circles relevant to the academic subject of the class being taught. Many students will feel more comfortable speaking up at first when a topic seems objective rather than personal.

But whatever the choice of your first circle, articulate the guidelines and be judicious about what questions you ask. Above all, remember to be clear about what you are doing and why. An IIRP trainer warns:

> I've heard this a number of times: "I asked students to come up with something and it didn't work." Ultimately, teachers in that situation are killing time, and they're not buying into the reason for doing circles. That's evident in the way they present it. There's no attitude from the teacher that what they're doing is worthwhile. The tone isn't there; there's no structure. If there's just a vague idea and overly general instructions, kids don't know what to say and it becomes a platform for them to act silly.

By avoiding these pitfalls, you will find the circle easier to facilitate, and there is a greater chance it will be a positive experience.

Types of Circles

When planning a circle, there are three main types to consider:
> Sequential go-arounds
> Non-sequential circles
> Fishbowls

The *sequential go-around* has been the one discussed most so far in this book. This is a circle in which a question or discussion point is raised and students answer in turn, proceeding around the circle in either a clockwise or counterclockwise direction. A volunteer may offer to go first, answer the question and choose the direction to proceed (to the volunteer's left or right). The teacher may be the first to answer the question and choose the direction. Or a teacher may ask a certain student to begin. This may be a trusted student who is sure to set a good example for the class. A teacher may also prep one or more students privately to fill them in on what they are looking for and call on those students first. If a talking piece is used, it should be passed from person to person to signify whose turn it is to speak. (See page 36 for more about talking pieces.)

Believe it or not, deciding which way to go around the circle can be a sticky problem. The best thing to do is establish the direction of the circle before the first person speaks. This eliminates what one circle facilitator dubs the "50-50 syndrome." Even though the two people on either side of the first person to speak have a 50-50 chance of going next, they always look shocked when the person tells them they are going to have to speak. So, before answering, if the person tells them they are next, they and the rest of the people on that side of the circle have a moment to organize their thoughts.

Sequential go-around circles can be used for check-ins and check-outs, "getting-to-know-you" activities or as part of an academic lesson. The length of response may vary. A quick check-in could be run in a few minutes with each student saying just a few words. The circle may be stretched out, too, with students being given more time for complex responses. Often the first person to go will set the tone and model the expected length of response. This is why it can be a good idea for teachers to model the types of responses they are looking for. Issuing clear instructions includes being explicit about the amount of time you want to spend conducting a circle.

If a student asks to pass or asks for more time, either skip the student or gently ask them to participate. Forcing students to speak when they are unwilling is usually counterproductive.

On the other hand, set a positive tone by establishing an expectation of participation from the beginning and offering positive encouragement to students who are reluctant to speak. This reluctance usually results from fear and shyness rather than a desire to disrupt the circle process. Patiently waiting silently for a student to speak may be all the encouragement they need. Prompting can help. Another technique is to let a student ask a friend or other classmate to help them think of something to say. If one or more students do pass on their turn, make a point of remembering to return to those students before the circle is closed to give them a chance to speak.

One of the benefits of the sequential go-around is that it gives everyone a chance to speak and an opportunity for all voices to be heard. This can be particularly beneficial to quiet or shy students who may be less inclined to offer their own opinions, thoughts and feelings without being prompted. In the context of the circle, these students frequently begin to play a leadership role that would not emerge otherwise. As students become familiar with the circle process and as trust and mutual respect are established, students sometimes look to these quiet but perceptive students for insight when they recognize a need for their special points of view.

Applications of the sequential go-around are limitless. It is a great format for students to give feedback to one another. Here again is an example of a high school teacher merging academic and personal goals. In this two-part circle students explored their personality traits with a look to what careers might best suit them:

> The first step in the circle was to have each student personally explain one of their strengths. After that was completed, they were to compliment the person to their right and identify one of their strengths as seen from a second person's perspective.
>
> Students were then guided into a personality/temperament test online, which they completed. Oddly enough, I had three students come to me and say that the perspective of their classmates was more in line with the test than their own perception. That simple circle led to additional discussions about how we perceive ourselves as well as those around us.

This type of question is a meatier alternative to simpler "get-to-know-you" questions, like "What pet do you have or want?" or "How do you spend your free time?" Other examples include: "What is one thing the person to your left is good at?" or "Talk about something someone did in class this week that helped you and that you appreciated." Student-to-student feedback questions build relationships in a class, help reinforce positive behavior that contributes to learning and teach students constructive ways of communicating with one another.

A teacher may also anticipate problems and nip them in the bud using the sequential go-around. Typical questions include: "What is one thing you can do today to ensure a successful class?" "How have you supported or what could you do to support a fellow student who is struggling to stay focused?" and "What can I as your teacher do to help make the science experiment run more smoothly this week?" More generally, teachers may simply ask students to state any concerns they have about an activity, homework assignment, test or class.

Non-sequential circles are more freely structured than sequential go-arounds. Conversation proceeds from one person to another in no fixed order. This type of circle allows a discussion to evolve organically and can be used effectively for problem solving as well.

Students only speak when they have something to say. How each speaker is determined is the defining feature of the non-sequential circle, which may be highly structured, loosely structured or unstructured.

Ground rules should be established at the beginning so everyone understands the format. A talking piece may be used in a non-sequential way to help keep order. Students may be required to raise their hands when they want to speak so the teacher or a student facilitator can then recognize one person at a time. In some groups, students may be allowed to call out or chime in at an appropriate moment without being formally recognized to speak.

The format will vary depending on the activity. If, for example, the class is brainstorming ideas for a skit or some other project, students may be permitted to call out their responses while someone writes everything down on a board. A teacher may also ask in a casual way, "Does anyone want to share their reaction to the activity we just did?" or "Would anyone like to bring up difficulties or challenges they had with the homework?" and wait for responses.

The amount of structure also depends on the maturity level of the students in a given group. Are they able to have a civil discussion with few rules or do they need stricter guidelines? The teacher must use their own judgment to decide which format will work best.

The major disadvantage of the non-sequential circle is that, unlike in the sequential go-around, not everyone is guaranteed a chance to speak. Non-sequential circles require more careful facilitation to ensure that all voices have a chance to be heard and that no one person or group of people dominates.

In some situations, you may trust that those who do not speak up are still benefiting from listening to the discussion. In other cases, the teacher might want to hear from everyone. One solution is simply to ask who has not spoken and explain that you would like to hear from everyone. You might also ask why some people have not spoken, which could be illuminating.

Alternatively, if not everyone has participated, a concluding sequential go-around may be conducted. Ask, for example, "What is one thing you learned, realized or were surprised by about this discussion?" This way everyone gets a chance to speak and put some closure to the activity.

Fishbowls are an effective way to use circles with a larger number of participants. The fishbowl allows participants in the inner circle to be active participants, while those in the outer circle act as observers (see Figure 5). Fishbowls can be structured entirely for the observers' benefit so that they can observe a specific process or certain interactions. They can also be set up for the participants' benefit, allowing observers to share their feedback at the end of the activity. The fishbowl may also comprise a combination of these two structures:

A high school teacher of a human sexuality class used a series of fishbowl exercises that allowed the observers in the outer circle to get a peek into the world of the participants on the inside. First he ran a fishbowl with the girls in the inner circle and the boys in the outer circle. The boys wrote down questions they wanted the girls to answer. The teacher drew them out of a hat, discarding or rewording any that weren't appropriate. The girls talked only to each other, responding to the boys' questions while the boys silently looked on.

Then the teacher flipped it around and the girls wrote questions that the boys answered as if they were in the locker room talking to each other. The class ended with one big circle where people gave feedback about how everyone had treated each other during the exercises.

The students kept asking to do this activity again, and the teacher decided to use the fishbowl for other topics as the year went on.

A common variation of the fishbowl leaves one chair empty in the inner circle. Only those on the inner circle are permitted to speak, so this allows those in the outer circle to leave their seats and sit in the empty chair to make a brief comment and contribute to the discussion. They then return to their original seats, leaving the empty chair available to anyone else who wishes to participate. Interestingly, the empty chair helps keep the focus in a large group, because even if members of the outer circle do not use the empty chair, the fact that they could if they wanted helps them pay more attention to the activity.

The principal of a small alternative high school describes how a fishbowl was used to create a meaningful ritual for a student who graduated mid-year:

> The best circle story I have is our circle for graduation. We had a student who was a January graduate. It is hard to do a formal ceremony for one student, so we decided to do a circle format. We invited everyone who was significant for this student, including his parents, family members, probation officer, caseworker and students who were close to him. Those people all sat in a center circle with the rest of our school community "fishbowling" that inner circle. We presented the diploma, and each person in the inner circle gave the student feedback about how proud they were and what they hoped for his future. We had an empty chair so that other members of the community could come in and give him feedback. This was the most heartfelt, emotional graduation that I have ever been a part of. We all talk about how we wish we could do that for every graduate.

Fishbowls may also be used for a technique called "restorative problem solving." Here a person offers to present a problem for consideration and selects a group of friends and trusted participants to sit in the inner circle, leaving one seat empty. The person spends a few minutes describing the problem. A feedback period follows, during which people in the inner circle and anyone from the outer circle who would like to occupy the empty chair tell the person what they think about the problem and offer thoughts and ideas.

The person receiving feedback must not respond to the suggestions until the end. A crucial rule of brainstorming, which was developed in the 1950s by Madison Avenue executive Alex Osborn, requires people to refrain from criticizing suggestions during the brainstorming process. This ensures that everyone feels comfortable contributing ideas. Though researchers have cast doubt on whether brainstorming is really more productive than other techniques for solving problems, brainstorming continues to be recognized for its strength as a team-building activity. When people comment on each other's suggestions and say things like, "I tried that" or "I don't think that will work," people begin to clam up. Allowing people to generate a creative flow of ideas without judgment makes for a more inclusive environment. Even silly suggestions are acceptable and can make the process more fun.

FISHBOWL CIRCLE
Figure 5

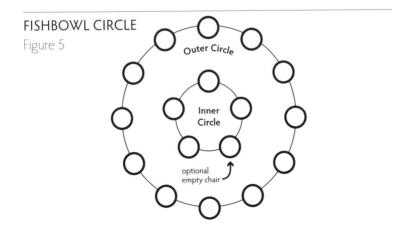

The person listening, while asked not to comment, may choose to write down what is said or appoint someone else as scribe. At the very end the person may say one or two things they will try, again without editorial comment. This process may be used in the class-room or in the staff room.

A creative, proactive use of restorative problem solving would be exploring the issues involved in completing a big project or term paper. One student, who is concerned about the assignment, could be asked to volunteer to present their fears and concerns about the project and ask for help. Trusted classmates could form the inner circle, with an empty seat left for those remaining in the outer circle to contribute if they have something to say. The feedback and assistance offered would be of use to the class as a whole, since all the students may confront similar problems associated with the assignment.

Talking Pieces

Many circle facilitators find a "talking piece" a useful tool for keeping students' attention focused and maintaining smoothly run circles. A talking piece can be any object that may be safely passed around the circle. The special-education teacher who was quoted on page 21 uses various toys and action figures as talking pieces (for which she says she is "famous" among her students). A practical item readily found in the classroom, like a chalkboard eraser or a pencil box, may be used. The talking piece may also be a symbolic object with meaning to the group or class. A small globe might be used as a talking piece in a geography class, or, more whimsically, a Shakespeare action figure could be used in an English literature class. Students, too, can be engaged to help choose the talking piece for a given class or discussion.

The primary rule of the talking piece is that whoever has it in their hands is the only one in the circle who is permitted to speak. The exception to this is when the teacher or facilitator needs to make a comment or ask a clarifying question. The talking piece is a great way of reinforcing the fact that only one person may speak at a time. It is a physical reminder that the person talking should receive the group's full attention. An additional benefit of the talking piece is that it may give fidgety students something tactile to handle and calm them while it is their turn to speak.

During a sequential go-around, the talking piece may be passed around the circle from person to person. In a non-sequential circle, the rules may vary. When a speaker finishes they may hand the talking piece to someone else, or else to a facilitator who hands the talking piece to the next speaker. Or the talking piece may be placed in the center of the circle and whoever wants to speak can walk to it and take it. It doesn't matter how it's done, as long as the rules are clear and its use facilitates a more orderly circle process.

Some people may feel uncomfortable presenting a talking piece to students to use in a circle, thinking it's only for young children and that older students will make a joke of it. But talking pieces have been used with people of all ages. The confidence of the facilitator in making the presentation will have a huge impact on how children receive the instructions and carry them out.

Check-in and Check-out

Check-in and check-out circles are some of the most common types of circles used in schools. As the names imply, check-in and check-out circles happen at the beginning and end of an activity or period of time, such as a class, day, week or marking period. If a check-in circle is held, it is not necessary to run a check-out circle and vice versa, though many teachers will do this, particularly if time permits. Check-in and check-out circles may deal with interpersonal or academic issues or both. A restorative practices specialist reported:

> In Toronto, Ontario, Canada, students in ninth grade are required to take French, but many do not like the obligatory class. A teacher with two sections of students at the

general academic level took some restorative practices classes and began using morning check-in and check-out circles as part of her teaching. By mid-semester she realized the students had become more focused and less challenging than she'd experienced with similar students in the past.

When the teacher was absent, the students said they missed her and they missed the circles. There were fewer behavior problems in these classes, and students were no longer being sent to the office. A year and a half later, kids were saying they loved the class, whereas in the past many complained they hated French and didn't want to be there.

A math teacher in the same school also started using check-in and check-out circles during his 75-minute block class, with a similar response. The kids became so much more focused that they were covering in just four days the material they used to cover in five, even though they were taking about 15 minutes per day for circles. Fridays regularly became a day for more circles and weekly review.

This large school of 2,000 students in Toronto serves a diverse community lacking communal connections, as people tend not to know one another. These stories helped move the whole school toward the use of restorative practices.

A *check-in* circle may be held at the beginning of the day in an elementary school or at the beginning of a class at higher levels. It can be short or long, but it tends to be a quick activity that should take only a few minutes. Some examples of questions for a check-in circle include:

> - How are you feeling today?
> - What was a highlight or a low point of your weekend?
> - What's something you're looking forward to in school this week?
> - What was the biggest challenge for you in completing your homework?

> What steps have you made in working on your project?
> What's something you need to have a successful day, class, week?

A check-in may also incorporate several questions. One might be personal, another academic and a third interpersonal. For instance, "How did you spend your evening, what is something you enjoyed learning about yesterday, and who is someone you want to spend time working with on an assignment today?" If the teacher or a trusted student models a concise response to the three questions and the other students follow suit, an activity like this can be completed in five minutes, and a good amount of information will have been shared in that time.

The check-in circle may also be used to follow up on agreements students have made about their behavior and academic goals. During a check-in, students may announce any agreements or plans they have, report whether they've kept to them and ask for assistance if needed. For instance, after lunch and recess a check-in could be held where students who have had trouble during these times in the past announce whether they had any problems that day and how they handled any problems that arose. Other students may offer feedback, assistance and suggestions.

Likewise, the *check-out* group may be academically or interpersonally oriented, and may provide students an opportunity to report on their ability to successfully stick to agreements during a certain period of time. Some possible check-out questions include:

> What was your favorite thing about today?
> What are you looking forward to today, this evening or this weekend?
> Give a compliment to someone for something they did well this week.
> Talk about one of your academic goals and how you furthered that in class.

There is no right or wrong way to use check-in and check-out circles. Some teachers use them every day, others on a certain day of the week. One teacher reports:

> We do check-in circles each Monday and "week in review" circles on Friday. Check-in is simply how the weekend was, any problems we can help with, any movies seen and so forth. "Week in review" is strictly academic. "How are your grades? What must improve? What teacher do you need to talk to?"
>
> Whenever a long-term assignment is given, I meet with students in a circle at the beginning, the middle and due date to discuss "wins and losses" during the process. In the "hot seat," during the last two to three minutes of class, one student sits in front of the room and receives compliments from the other students. This builds family.

The check-in and check-out are commonly used in other settings as well. A residential school conducts check-in circles every day when students return to their housing at the end of the academic day. The question can be as simple as "How was your day?" or "What do you need this evening?" The circle might take place over snacks at the kitchen table and be as short as five minutes or as long as a half hour. Other discussion points include arranging time for doing homework assignments and coordinating chores and recreational activities.

Check-in and check-out circles can be used in teacher's meetings, too. A useful question might be "What's one way you have used circles effectively in your classroom?" A ten-minute go-around of this kind gives everyone new ideas for their own classes. (More ideas of how circles can be used among staff will be discussed in Chapter 5.)

Integrating Circles with Course Content

While many people use circles for problems alone and believe circles are something that happens only when educational goals are impeded, it is undoubtedly clear by now that we advocate the integration of circles into the basic structure of teaching.

Teachers have many different means and techniques for delivering course content, including lectures, small group activities, discussions, tests and quizzes, videos, projects and games. Think of the circle as adding another string to a teacher's bow, a versatile technique capable of serving multiple functions. Here a teacher structured a circle to introduce a new topic, gauge student interest and give students ownership of the upcoming unit of study:

> After an exam at the conclusion of a marking period, a teacher said to her students, "Next semester we'll be study-ing government. What things would you like to know about that subject?"
>
> One boy said he wanted to learn about political parties, another student said she wanted to learn about the political process and how laws are made, and a third said he wanted to know more about the election process.
>
> The conversation took on a life of its own. In fact, the enthusiasm surprised the teacher. She wrote down every-thing the students wanted to learn and explained that she would incorporate all these subjects into the unit on gov-ernment. Students enjoyed the discussion so much they didn't want to leave class when the period was over.

Natural uses of the circle in the classroom arise organically from a combined understanding of the nature of the circle and the subject material to be covered in a class:

> A grammar school in England uses circles regularly when introducing new subjects. The teacher writes a word or draws a picture on the board and asks students to "Say

one thing you know about this subject." The subject might be computers, Romans, the seasons or the difference between tropical, polar and temperate climates. In math class, students recite their multiplication tables going around the circle, and younger students practice counting forwards and backwards. Basics, like the days of the week, months of the year, shapes, telling time and directions — left, right, clockwise, counterclockwise — may be practiced in the circle. Coordination skills are reinforced with games involving a small ball or doing "the wave" around the circle. Students may also be assigned "talking partners" — the person sitting next to them in the circle, perhaps — and report back to the whole circle what they have discussed.

Using a circle to present and process the subject at hand engages students in what they are learning. In a Singapore high school, foreign-language teachers use circles so students can practice conversation. An American social studies department uses a circle to process students' emotional responses to a subject that is studied in every school in the United States. A teacher wrote:

In world cultures we have designed lessons around the use of circles. For example, in the past when we learned about the African slave trade the students would take part in many activities to demonstrate what Africans went through during this time. The students always enjoyed the lesson; however, it was not until we incorporated the circle principle into the lesson that it became the most powerful. At the conclusion of their activities (slave march, Middle Passage journey and Amistad scene), students were placed in a circle and were asked to discuss the emotions they felt during these activities. The response was overpowering. Each student was able to share their anger, frustration and remorse about what these Africans had to endure during this time. Students had always shared what they thought, but the circle allowed each student to display and express their emotions. It changed the way we teach that lesson.

Any time a discussion is sought, a circle may provide the most useful framework for facilitating positive interchange between students. There's an assessment component, as well. Like written assignments and quizzes, circles provide a way for teachers to measure students' comprehension of a subject.

Behavioral Expectations

Discussing behavioral expectations at the beginning of a term, before commencing a class project, or before boarding the bus to go on a field trip are truly proactive uses of the circle process. When students articulate their own needs and desires for behavior in a class, as well as rationales for those expectations, they take ownership and feel responsible for sticking to and even helping uphold the rules. Often the rules or needs expressed by students will be similar to those desired by the teacher. Of course the teacher can help fill in the gaps and add to the ideas that students express.

Students may write the expectations on poster boards and post them in the classroom. This makes it possible for teachers to refer to those expectations as a reminder to children of the behavioral guidelines they helped come up with. Students themselves will frequently take the responsibility to police themselves and point to the behavioral expectations to ask other students to change what they are doing. This is because students often don't like when other students misbehave, but previously they haven't known what to do about it and may not want to "tell on" other students. The behavioral expectations developed in the circle provide a framework for students to take responsibility.

A similar approach can be used before an assembly, a field trip or a visit by a guest speaker or other visitor to the class. In a circle, ask students what are appropriate ways to behave in a particular circumstance, and then ask students to anticipate ways they might get into trouble. Students may be asked to identify what they can do if they feel they want to act out in a certain way and what they will do to remedy a problem if something does come up.

Notice that here we are discussing problems, but we are doing it proactively. By airing issues beforehand you dispel many potential problems. By talking about what might go wrong there is less chance of children actually acting out. If and when students do act out, remind them of their own words and ask them to keep their commitments to behave. And remember that when things do go wrong, a responsive circle may then be used to resolve the problem. But that is a subject for the next chapter.

A slightly different twist to this whole idea is found in the example of the teacher who begins his classes each year with a circle called "Ten Things I Need To Know About You (in order to be your teacher)," which he describes as a community builder. This activity serves as an icebreaker and helps bridge the distance between the teacher and his students. The same concept could be adapted to a project or field trip. "What are ten things I need to know about you in order for us to have a successful [fill in the blank]?" Finding new ways to present circles will keep them fun and interesting, as well as useful.

Games

Everyone has played group games with people seated in a circle. "Duck, Duck, Goose" is one of the first games many of us played as children and is widely known, but the list of circle games is long, and most people can name at least a few. Examples of games can easily be found in books or by searching online. Rather than focus too much on specific games, we'll focus instead on some of the features of games that make them useful to classroom teachers, as well as on guidelines that will help teachers have success in their classes playing circle games.

Games can be used as group-building activities, as icebreakers and as trust activities. An English teacher used a game the first day of class for students to learn each other's names. They made up alliterative names for themselves, like "Super Steve" and "Jivin' Jen" and walked around the class introducing one another in an attempt to recall each other's names. The activity itself was a success, but the students continued to use the names all year long. The teacher was shocked that something so silly created lasting bonds for the class that year. Nor did the students forget the meaning of the term "alliteration."

Games may be used to creatively cover academic material. One teacher created a circle game for reviewing material before tests. She asks the class multi-answer questions, like "Name the seven continents" and "List the countries in Europe that border Germany." The students raise their hands to answer, and when a ball is tossed to them they shout out the answers. The children are engaged, they have fun, and they review class material all at once.

As with any circle, games will be most successful when the goals and rules of the game are clearly stated at the beginning of the circle. Part of the introduction may consist of asking students for input into what is appropriate behavior during a game.

After the game has been played, it is often a great idea to process the game with a circle go-around. "Did you like the game? Why or why not?" "What did you get out of this experience?" "What changes would you make the next time we play a game like this?" By building in this kind of feedback loop everyone has a chance to take responsibility for the activity, and often students will offer suggestions to make the game even better next time.

If a game is not going well, remember that it is perfectly acceptable to simply pull the plug and end the game. Games are meant to build relationships, not to undo or destroy them. If something doesn't feel right, simply stop the game. You may decide to have a circle go-around to process what has happened. A question might be "What is something I could have done differently to make this game go better?" It is also okay to say, "This isn't working. We're going to move on to the rest of our day, and we'll try this again tomorrow."

Other Proactive Circles

Once you start using circles, ideas for using them will multiply, especially when teachers in a school start exchanging ideas.

A teacher used a circle to review for a test. The question she presented to the class was "What are you worried about?" Students started saying, "I don't understand this part" and "I don't understand that part." Other students began explaining what they understood of the questions students raised, and they helped each other fill in the gaps. The circle turned into a student-driven review, and everyone got behind the activity.

In a high school in Singapore, students were asked, "What can be done to improve the school?" and the feedback was delivered to the administration. Two suggestions that were acted upon were improved ventilation in some of the facilities and a school talent show.

In Jamaica, students are learning to use circles to build community in a country riddled with violence. The goal is to build interpersonal relationships and thoughtfulness and explore feelings. A couple of questions that have been used in these circles for elementary school students include: "Did you ever get blamed for something you really didn't do?" and "Talk about something you've done that you felt badly about."

Saying goodbye is another great use of the circle. Endings are often abrupt and leave people feeling at a loss. A circle ceremony helps soften the ending by acknowledging change and providing an opportunity for parting words to be spoken. If a student moves away mid-year or a teacher cannot complete a term because of pregnancy, surgery or some other reason, a circle can provide an opportunity to exchange feedback between the people staying and the person leaving. At the end of the year, goodbyes may be said in a circle, using questions like, "The thing I will miss most about this school year will be ..." or "Now that school is over I'm looking forward to ..." A circle may be used to tie a bow on an extracurricular activity that ends mid-year. When a concert or play is concluded or a sports season is over, students may be invited to participate in a circle to express their appreciation to the teacher or coach who runs an activity and reflect on their experiences with one another.

In a residential school for at-risk youth, a proactive circle is held a few weeks before a student returns to their home and community. While this is not a formal FGDM conference (as explained in Chapter 2), some of the elements are similar. The circle focuses on anticipating problems and planning for the child's return home in order to ensure success and avoid a repeat of the problems that led to the student's placement in the school in the first place. The residential counselor invites the family to the circle, and everyone gets a chance to talk about their fears, rules that need to be put in place and how things will look for the child back at home.

Similarly, counselors in a Costa Rican high school held circles with students who failed the year and needed to repeat a grade:

> The counselors held a series of circles with four students and a parent of each, generally a mother, with a total of 10 people per group. The participants were asked to talk about how they felt about the youth failing the year, what they might do differently next year and what support they needed.
>
> The most powerful effect, according to the counselors, was seeing the mothers talk and listen to each other. They shared how much they loved their children and how afraid they were of not knowing how to handle the situation. They were comforted to know that they all had similar fears and doubts. They also expressed a willingness to support one another.

Three More Points

The shape of the circle is important. Sometimes the shape of the room is awkward or students seat themselves behind other students or outside the circle. Don't be afraid to ask people to move or to rearrange the circle so everyone can see and be seen. This is crucial to creating a level playing field where everyone feels safe and included. The shape, too, can have a subtle effect, so try to maintain a circle if at all possible.

Trust the circle. Occasionally a circle takes a surprising turn, but the result can still be very useful. A teacher wrote:

> An example of a circle taking on its own life was in a lesson about mistakes. I know I posed the questions incorrectly. It was meant to be, "Can you give me an example of a financial mistake which you'd like to take back?" I'm not sure how it came out, but students began sharing about family structure, lost relatives, friends, relationships, divorce and so forth. Students were extremely supportive of one another, offered advice and helped each other through the emotions. It was really neat to see and experience.

The circle is a container that is strong enough to hold just about anything that is poured into it. Discover what is possible.

Circles encourage problem solving. Finally, remember that the proactive use of circles establishes them as a powerful tool for dealing with problems later on. As you grow comfortable using circles and as a group of students gets to know one another throughout the course of a year, go deeper with circles. An IIRP trainer summarizes the proactive use of circles and argues that teachers should think in terms of an 80/20 distribution between proactive and responsive use:

> Eighty percent of circles should be proactive. That means

using circles to be collaborative, to engage students and to get their input and opinions on things.

Use circles to discuss course content, whether that's sharing work in a circle format, responding to and sharing thoughts about a story or the lesson or asking for input and support from other students. You can get students to ask one another for assistance to help them complete their work.

You can also discuss norms for the class early on in the year or term, such as expectations for assignments or expected norms of behavior in the class. This is all in addition to the trust builders, icebreakers and getting-to-know-you activities people automatically associate with circles.

The other 20 percent of circles may be responsive. But it is by doing all those other things on a consistent, regular, frequent, daily basis that people learn the skills, build the trust and have the confidence they need to effectively respond to problems and deal with larger, more important issues.

When issues arise, lean on the social capital that has been built through the use of circles. Problems then become opportunities, and the classroom becomes a functioning unit.

CHAPTER 4

Responsive Circles

An assistant principal of a high school in a major U.S. city on the federal government's mandated list of persistently dangerous schools used the circle process to deal with an ongoing problem in an art class for upperclassmen. Two hallways on either side of the art room were used by students as a shortcut, even when class was in session. The young and inexperienced art teacher was intimidated by the constant disruptions and resulting misbehavior of students in her class. They refused to do work and pay attention, and they listened to music on headphones. There were frequent shoving matches, teasing incidents and boys overtly flirting with girls. The situation was out of control, and a lot of students were angry about the class.

The problem came to a head when a resource officer (a police officer stationed in the school) who was new to the school walked into the classroom and immediately called the assistant principal. He said, "Please come to the art class right away! It's been ransacked." He thought there had been a riot. The assistant principal said sardonically, "No, that's the way the class always looks." Even though circles were new to the school and he had never run one, the assistant principal was determined to try.

Although IIRP trainers would have advised him to get a couple of students as allies to help start the circle off appropriately, he courageously plunged ahead. He used a ball as a talking piece, and at first the kids jokingly tossed it around the room. The assistant principal was persistent and let the students know this wasn't a joke. He intended to get to the bottom of what was going on. Finally, when the students realized that the assistant principal meant to create an environment to solve the problems, not simply to identify the culprits and mete out punishments, they opened up and began talking about what had been happening in the crazy classroom.

One student, however, absolutely refused to participate in the discussion. The assistant principal addressed him directly and said, "I need everyone to contribute to this. What is it you are willing to do? I'm not giving up." The boy remained defiant. He answered, "I ain't gonna say nothin'!" and threw the ball on the ground. The assistant principal remained calm and echoed the boy, "So, you're committed to saying nothing." Another student was so frustrated by the boy's refusal to participate, he picked up the ball and yelled at his fellow student, "You're the f***in' problem!"

The assistant principal, while relieved that another student was calling this boy to task for his contribution to the problem, asked the students to confront one another appropriately. He redirected the discussion to the issue of why the art class was important to students and what impact the boy's behavior had on them. Students talked about their love of art, their need to complete the course for graduation, their career goals and other things.

At a certain point, one student said to the boy who was causing a lot of trouble, "You know, I think you're really funny. But you do this stuff every day. That makes it impossible to do the class."

Amazingly, the boy who was causing a lot of the trouble raised his hand and asked for the ball. He said, "When I do this stuff you guys laugh at me and that encourages me to keep it up." At that point, the class period ended, but the assistant principal knew he was on to something, so he gave the students passes out of their next class and moved the circle to an empty classroom. Keeping an entire class of students from going to their next class was a pretty big decision, but the assistant principal believed it was warranted given the extent of the ongoing problems and the progress being made in the circle.

As the conversation continued, students brought up the fact that they felt the activities they were doing in class were beneath them, that they weren't being challenged. This came as a shock to the teacher, who said, "I tried to do more advanced things, but you destroyed the materials, you threw them around, and a lot of students refused to participate." The students admitted to this. The teacher said she'd only be willing to try those things again if the students would make a commitment to support each other to behave maturely and respect the materials. The students agreed and said they really wanted to do sculpture.

The circle culminated with the students developing a detailed plan for turning the class around. They talked about ways to support the "funny" student behaving himself, made a commitment to respect the art materials and take their work seriously, and described how they would work together to keep students from using the classroom as a shortcut between hallways.

Finally, the teacher said, "I will teach you sculpture, but I want you to keep your commitment to respect each other and the art materials." The circle ended, and the next week the class started their sculpture unit. On the first day, when some students tried to use the classroom as a hallway, the whole class confronted them: "Hey, this is our class. Stay out of here!" Before long, people stopped trying to cut through the room, the "funny" student got his clowning under control, and the class began to function as an art class.

In this story, the positive desires of the students to have a functioning art class overcame resistance on the part of some of the students and the inexperience of the staff. Normally, problem circles should not be attempted until students have been familiarized with the circle process by means of proactive circles. However, the facilitator had the right attitude and was persistent. He treated the misbehavior in the classroom as a symptom of unaddressed issues, and he engaged the students in a process that resulted in the class bonding together to solve its own problems.

In the following story, again an assistant principal at a U.S. high school attempted to use a circle without having done the preliminary work of familiarizing students with circles first. This time the results were dismal:

An assistant principal who had received some training in the use of circles decided to put what he'd learned to the test at 2 p.m. one afternoon, less than an hour before the end of the school day. He had his secretary announce the names of 15 students over the loudspeaker to the entire school. Since no classrooms were available, the students were told to report immediately to the wrestling room. Because they were all notorious troublemakers, no one in the school doubted the students were about to receive some kind of punishment.

In the hot and stuffy wrestling room, the assistant principal arranged the students in a circle and said, "All right, I want to know how you guys are going to get your act together and change." The assistant principal cared about the students, but he didn't realize that calling them out this way humiliated them. Plus, the time and setting were all wrong. On top of that, another staff member who was present delivered a blistering lecture to the students before any of them had a chance to say a word.

The assistant principal was trying to take a firm stand with these students, and he believed the circle would be a way to help the students take responsibility for their actions and be supported to make positive changes. But the way the circle was organized set a punitive tone that made the students belligerent and uncooperative. They muttered their displeasure and made jokes about the circle. Some kids pretended to fall asleep. Nothing productive took place, and the whole thing disintegrated into chaos. Finally, the assistant principal had to let the kids go home without anything positive to show for the effort.

When people learn about circles, they often say, "Let's put all the worst problem kids together and deal with them using a circle." There are two major problems with this approach. By segregating the problem students, you stigmatize them. In effect, you are saying that they are not part of the larger school community, when what you really want to do is integrate them, let them know that they matter and that their behavior affects everyone.

Secondly, this segregated approach intentionally excludes the overwhelming majority of the student population, who actually want to see things go well and will support that happening. The circle in the art class is a great example of this. Even though a lot of students contributed to the problems in that class, deep down many students were unhappy with the situation and wanted to see the class go well. The pressure they brought to bear on their class-mates made finding a solution possible.

This is not to say that circles are ineffective with difficult students: precisely the opposite. This chapter includes a number of examples of circles held in alternative school settings serving the most challenging youth in their communities, including many who have been expelled or excluded from public high schools, convicted of criminal behavior and deemed ungovernable. Even in these settings, however, facilitators build a positive sense of community and cultivate student leadership before using circles to confront specific misbehaviors. For those who doubt the potential of circles for making a difference with their students, these examples demonstrate that circles have been tested in the most challenging situations.

Something Happened in Class

Many things can disrupt a class: someone having destroyed property; students teasing or bullying one another; students talking too much during a lesson; half the class not doing their homework; people cheating on a test or copying each other's assignments; items disappearing; someone cursing at a teacher; a person making a sexual or racial slur; a group of students arriving late to class for the umpteenth time. While these problems can be handled in a variety of ways, a circle enlists the entire class in a process of positive change.

As with proactive circles, preparation and presentation are the keys to successful responsive circles. The intention of the circle and the way you frame the problem shapes the circle and influences your ability to achieve a desirable outcome:

A counselor in an alternative school thought up a new activity, which she was excited to present to her students. However, rather than being good sports, the students complained and mocked the activity. The counselor felt angry and wanted to yell. Instead, she stopped the class, put everyone in a circle and did a feelings check. She asked students to briefly explain how they were feeling, and most of them said they felt angry.

When it was the teacher's turn to speak, she said, "I'm really hurt, and this is why." She explained how she'd put time and effort into developing the activity, had been excited to try it out but was hurt by the students' complaints and jokes. When the students heard how their mocking affected the teacher, they sympathized with her and redid the activity with a positive attitude.

The counselor's instinct was to yell at the students. Her

training in restorative practices indicated a different approach. She let everyone air their feelings, including herself. The circle took a few minutes and the group got back on track without a need to assign blame or punish anyone.

The counselor, now an administrator at an IIRP model school, lists three main areas of focus for any responsive circle:

1. Think about what was happening in the class that wasn't working, and have people take responsibility for what they were doing to contribute to that behavior.

2. Ask what kind of atmosphere students and teachers ideally want in the classroom.

3. Reflect and think about what each person is going to do to help attain that ideal.

A responsive circle may address one, two or all three of these components. In the following story, all three areas got addressed, though in a roundabout order:

During a science class a student sprayed hand sanitizer into a fish tank that contained a frog — a class pet — but no one knew (or admitted that they knew) who had done it. Instead of worrying about finding the culprit, however, the teacher held a problem-solving group on the issue of how to keep the frog safe. The students came up with a list of rules. They discussed how to handle the frog carefully. The class wrote up a poster board above the tank to explain the rules, including what you can and can't do with the frog and how to ask for permission to play with him.

When the student who sprayed the sanitizer realized he wasn't going to get in trouble in the normal way, he admitted to the teacher that he had been the one who sprayed the sanitizer in the tank. His consequence was a natural one: he had to help clean out the tank, which made him feel proud.

When a wrongdoer restores his good name and standing by taking responsibility for his actions, the restorative process has clearly been successful. But note, too, that if that student hadn't accepted responsibility for spraying the hand sanitizer, the circle still would have been a success. When you frame a circle to resolve a problem rather than catch a culprit, you address the relevant issues and achieve desirable results.

Occasionally, students become so facile with the use of circles that they initiate circles themselves:

> In a classroom in the first suburban ring outside a major U.S. city, students in a mostly African-American class interpreted something their white teacher had said as racially offensive. Word spread throughout the school, and the teacher was at a loss as to how to address the issue.
>
> Two seniors came to the teacher during that class. They said they'd heard there was a problem, and they asked to run a circle. The teacher agreed and actually left the class in their hands while he went into the hallway for ten minutes. He had no idea what was being said until the two seniors came out and said, "They're ready for you."
>
> The teacher sat in the circle and the students did a go-around. Each of them said they realized the teacher meant no offense, but that they wanted to express their feelings about what they thought he'd meant. The teacher acknowledged that he understood how his remark could have been taken the wrong way. After that, the class got back on track.

The more experience you gain using circles, and the more you trust your instincts, the further you can go. You begin to understand that almost anything that comes up can be used to address the real issues going on in a class:

The IIRP trained the entire teaching staff at an urban elementary/middle school in the use of circles. The trainer returned to the school a few weeks later to follow up, and a sixth-grade teacher asked for help. She just couldn't see how to run circles with her students. She didn't think they could do it, and she was wary of their negative attitudes. As soon as the trainer walked into the room, one child gave him a dirty look. Another muttered something about the trainer to two other children, who both snickered.

The class formed a circle, and the trainer asked the class for permission to speak. He said, "I'm a visitor, and I want to talk about what it was like to come into this classroom. I said, 'Hi,' and no one answered me. I'm not going to confront this, but I want you to know it feels uncomfortable. Now, how I feel is not a big concern. But I wonder what it's like to be a student in this class and how you feel about how you treat each other."

The students did a circle go-around and talked about how they felt about their class. Children said people were really disrespectful. One said he was afraid to speak up in class because he'd get teased. A couple of students said they really wanted to do well but that there was so much talking they got distracted very easily. Some admitted they were the ones who disrupted the class. By way of excuse, they said they didn't really want to be mean to anybody, they just wanted to be funny.

The trainer asked, "What's one thing you can do to change some of the things you don't like?" Students said, "I'll come in and sit down and do work." Some said they would stop being goofy and talking all the time. Everyone said something. Both go-arounds took about 15 to 20 minutes total.

One child said, "If we're talking about all this stuff now, how are we going to remember this tomorrow?" One boy said, "Let's make a poster." A few students made a poster of the things people said they'd do and hung it in the class.

The trainer had begun the circle by saying how he felt when people ignored him and made jokes behind his back. But what really hooked the students was when he cut the lecture short and said the circle wasn't about him but about the students themselves. The children experienced a sense of ownership, believing that what they said mattered, and they began to take responsibility for making things better.

After the circle, the trainer urged the teacher to make good use of the poster the students made. She said, "How about I have the kids read it at the start of every class?" In that way she started to see how she could work with her students to manage the class and solve problems.

Singling Out Students

When misbehaving students disrupt a class, other students often have feelings about it. While a circle provides those who have done wrong an opportunity to take responsibility for their behavior and develop a plan for behaving differently, it may also give the other students a chance to tell how they feel. This helps clear the air and relieve feelings and frustrations the class may have.

But deciding whether to single out a student for his or her behavior in a circle process can be a difficult decision. Sometimes the attention will make a student feel ashamed or feel that the circle itself is a punishment, making matters worse. However, when a student's behavior has had an influence on other students, a circle empowers the class and gives them a chance to play a supporting role:

Students in a fifth-grade class in Canada were frustrated with a boy in their class with Asperger's syndrome, a high-functioning form of autism characterized by significant difficulties socializing and relating to peers. The boy's behavior became more problematic as the school year went on, and a major incident occurred mid-year when the boy, oblivious to the true danger of his actions, swung a baseball bat in the classroom and seriously frightened the rest of the children. He didn't intend to hurt anyone. In fact, he thought what he'd done was funny and that other people would agree. He couldn't understand why anyone would be upset about it.

The situation was complicated because the boy's parents didn't acknowledge the severity of the challenges the boy presented to the school, the teacher and the other children in the class. Therefore, the school could not rely on the parents to do something to curb the student's behavior. In the end, the principal and the teacher decided a circle would be the best way to confront the issue in a supportive way. The school's child-and-youth worker (school counselor in U.S. parlance) was called in to facilitate a circle using the basic restorative questions: What did you think when this happened? What was the hardest thing? What can we do to make it better? The students, teacher and principal all participated.

The first circle was not completely satisfying, so the facilitator conducted a total of three circles over a period of three weeks. During the second circle there was a feeling of change and movement. The Asperger's student seemed to acknowledge the effect of his actions a little more each time. By the third week, the other children said they had started to see a difference in his behavior and that they were feeling good about that.

After the three circles, the student with Asperger's syndrome presented no other serious problems during the rest of the school year. His behavior changed, but perhaps more significant, the other students understood him better. Their attitudes towards him improved, and they discovered other ways to act and speak to him to avoid conflicts.

The restorative practices specialist who relayed this anecdote said, "When you create an open environment where people can communicate, you create an environment where people don't get triggered to react without thinking. This is the power of the circle. It helps people work together in the community, as well as be safe."

In many of the situations presented so far in this chapter, circles have been employed at the front end to confront behaviors and solve problems. A slightly different approach is to arrange a circle *after* a teacher or principal has addressed a problem with an individual. For instance, a student who has misbehaved and been sent to the principal may, upon returning to class, inform other students about what has happened and ask for feedback. When a student hears from their peers how they feel about what they have done, it reinforces the need to make positive changes. The process helps reintegrate the misbehaving student into the class, and students are less likely to talk about a student behind their back when they've been informed about what has happened and spoken directly with that person.

The following example shows how this can be done. Here, a student in an emotional-support setting in a public school had to be hospitalized for his behavior. The teacher wrote:

> Tony was deliberately defiant with the staff and inten-
> tionally disrupted his peers as they attempted to complete
> a test, because he had been given a poor grade for failing to
> complete his homework. As the day went on, Tony's behav-
> ior became more and more uncontrollable. Even after
> almost two hours of counseling with his parents, social
> workers, therapists and teachers, Tony continued to engage
> in dangerous and threatening behavior until he was taken
> by ambulance to a hospital to be evaluated.

When he returned to school a few days later, Tony answered the Restorative Questions [explained in Chapter 2] and checked in with the community. At first he seemed reluctant to check in and was nonchalant about his behavior, accepting only limited responsibility. However, when his peers began answering the other set of Restorative Questions, relating to how they had been harmed, what they had thought about when the incident was happening, what impact it had on them, what had been the hardest thing for them and what they wanted to happen to make things right, it created an emotional outpouring.

Tony's peers told him how frustrated they were with his behavior and how embarrassed it had made them. They said they were afraid that their non-disabled peers would view them differently because they were in the same class with Tony, who had been taken away in an ambulance. One boy said he felt unsafe around Tony because of his behavior and because he wasn't sure how Tony would react to other situations.

The students' feedback left an indelible mark on Tony. He listened, then quietly left the circle to sit in a separate area of the classroom. After a short time, I went to talk to him alone and saw that he had been crying quietly. He said he hadn't realized how upset he'd made his peers and that he was embarrassed by his behavior. He decided to write a letter to each of his peers, apologizing for how they had been negatively affected. He also made a plan, which was posted on his desk and made known to all, about how he would handle his frustration the next time he was upset and would seek their help to do the right thing. This situation allowed the class to grow together as a community, be more comfortable expressing their feelings aloud, and hold each other accountable while still being supportive and willing to fix harms that occurred. (Webb, 2010)

Another time you might need to single out a student is if they are determined to disrupt a circle. As with any activity, the first step is to ask for the person's cooperation, and the second step is to remove the person from the circle:

In a high school classroom, a student was sent into the hall for disrupting a circle. The rest of the students talked about the student's behavior for a few minutes. The students did a go-around and said how funny the student was and how much they liked him, but, they said, he just never knew when to stop. They felt badly that he had to be excluded. Someone said, "What can we do?"

The class decided to invite the student back into the circle and start by telling him how they felt. The overwhelming message was, "You're funny, but you've got to learn when to stop." The class talked for a few minutes and everyone, including the boy, agreed upon a verbal cue they would use when the boy needed to be prompted to stop clowning. They would simply say, "You don't know when it's time to stop. Now it's time to stop." The teacher and students alike used the cue every time the boy crossed the line, and they reported that this really worked.

Any one person determined to disrupt or block an activity, be it lunch, recess, a class, or an assembly, can surely do so. The circle process itself won't always bring that person around, though often it does.

Another kind of circle issue that might arise is when one or more students refuse to participate in a circle. How you choose to handle this is a matter of judgment and circumstance. If your efforts to encourage or persuade them do not work, you must decide whether you are willing to provoke a power struggle with the student or if you would rather allow that student to sit outside the circle and observe. To ensure that they do not disrupt, ask these students to promise to sit quietly and refrain from speaking or doing anything to distract the other students. Make a big deal of this. You might even ask them to shake your hand to seal their promise to watch but not disturb. Here's an example of how this worked successfully:

Shortly after an alternative school in New York City began using restorative practices, a circle was convened to discuss a frightening incident of a bulletin board being set on fire, presumably by a student whose identity was never discovered. Four students refused to participate. The principal of the school ran the circle and allowed the four students to sit and watch after they'd made verbal commitments not to interrupt the process. The circle lasted several class periods and had to be moved to another room halfway through the process. When the circle reconvened in another classroom, the four students asked to join the circle and participated appropriately.

In another case, three girls started a conflict on the playground because they felt shy about their ability to dance with other girls at recess. A circle was held, and one of the girls kept disrupting the process. She was excluded from the circle and sent out of the room, allowing the other two girls to take a serious look at their behavior. Later, the disruptive girl was brought back into the room to have another chance, and she participated positively. Limit setting combined with positive peer pressure helped the circle conclude with a successful outcome.

Taken as a whole, the examples in this section demonstrate how one can treat students with respect and provide them with support, even while holding them accountable for their behavior. Achieving this balance is the goal of the restorative process.

Patterns of Behavior

Some issues that arise in class involve a large number of students or unidentified students. Circles may be framed to address these issues in a general way. The circle facilitator may choose to tackle such a problem either directly or indirectly.

For example, in an instance where a number of small items belonging to students, the teacher and the school kept disappearing over a period of time, the teacher did not know whether one person was stealing or whether a number of people were responsible. Perhaps the pattern of thefts broke down trust in the class, and students no longer respected one another's property.

To address the problem directly, the teacher first asked students to identify the items that were missing and how they felt about the situation. They followed this up by asking students what they thought could be done to address the problem. Often students come up with creative solutions that the teacher didn't think of, as in the case where students decided to hold a bake sale to raise money to replace stolen property. In this case, the culprit was never found. The fact that the class addressed the issue may have caused those who took the items to think twice before doing so again. Or perhaps those who knew which student or students were stealing but were not prepared to name those students, in light of hearing how their classmates felt, then pressured those responsible to stop.

The circle facilitator has a natural tendency to want to solicit information about who is to blame for causing a problem or to ask culprits to come forth. Since the latter rarely happens, such an approach may bring the circle process to a screeching halt. Waiting for culprits to come forth actually gives them power to steal time and energy from the group by remaining silent.

By all means encourage people to take responsibility, but the primary objective should be to explore how a negative pattern of behavior affects the majority of the class. Think of students as victims of the negative behavior. Give voice to those who want to see the class go well. The culprits will be forced to sit in the circle and listen to other students talk about their feelings. Even if the truth of the matter is never fully disclosed, the undesirable behavior often ceases after such circles.

As an alternative to the direct approach, you may choose to broach a topic indirectly. If there is an issue of racial tension in a class involving numerous students, a go-around question could be, "Have you ever felt uncomfortable because someone didn't like the color of your skin, the place you come from or something else about your background that you can't change?" Students may speak generally or end up discussing examples from the class. Of course, this conversation requires a certain amount of group trust, so you probably want to bring this up with students who are already comfortable with the circle process.

Other examples of indirect questions for raising issues include: Did you ever have something stolen from you, and how did that feel? How does it feel when you tease someone? What prevents you from being able to learn in a class? By turning the questions around, children begin to see issues from different perspectives.

Indirect questions help students get to know one another, and the resulting discussions have an impact on norms of behavior. When people talk about how they prefer to be treated and get to know each other better, they are less likely to hurt each other thoughtlessly.

If students respond positively to an indirect approach, the facilitator may then decide to ask people if they are willing to take responsibility for their own behavior. Teachers and their assistants may also choose to discuss things they could do to make the class run better. When adults make themselves vulnerable this way, they strengthen their relationships with students and provide a model for children to talk honestly about their own actions.

There are also times when an adult can't quite pin down what is happening in a class, but they intuitively know something is wrong. A negative tone or a hunch that something just isn't right is reason enough to call a circle and ask students to talk about how they are feeling. At a time like this, you might express your own sense that something is wrong and ask if anyone feels the same way. If students raise concerns, take it from there. If they don't, you may want to back off the issue for the time being. On the other hand, you may discover that students are preoccupied with worry about a big test in their next class or that something happened earlier in the day that hasn't been resolved. Take a few minutes for students to air their feelings and make suggestions for completing the class successfully. This usually changes the tone so you can continue teaching.

If a whole class has become unruly, as in the following situation where someone who was filling in for others lost control of the class, a circle can be used to restore order and cooperation. Every child in this group of 30 students played a part in creating a chaotic situation. Even so, the facilitator refused to assign blame. Instead, she adopted the premise that things had to be different, and she asked students what each of them would do to make that happen:

One day an alternative school administrator was supervising all 30 students at one of the school's several sites along with just one other staff member. The rest of the staff were absent for one reason or another, and the students took advantage of the situation. They ran away from the group activity they were doing and scattered throughout the school building. Kids used the computers and did anything they wanted, refusing to follow directions. The administrator was shocked and scared. She didn't know what to do at first, because nothing quite like that had ever happened to her before.

After she regained her bearings, the administrator and the other staff member managed to lure students one by one back to the main room. She said to herself, "Okay, this is never going to happen again." She said to the group, seated in a circle once again, "Who wants to have a good afternoon?" All the students agreed except for one, so she said he could sit quietly and not participate. She then asked the rest of the students, "What needs to happen to have a good afternoon? What do you need to do? We trust that whatever you say you'll be true to your word."

Believe it or not, the students responded positively to this. The administrator reported, "The day went from disaster to these kids having so much fun." The planned activity commenced, and the students said, "We want to do it outside." It was such a beautiful day that the staff agreed. When the students realized the activity wasn't working, they insisted on going back inside to make it a success, even though the staff told them they were willing to come up with a different activity that would work better outdoors.

The administrator — in the role of substitute teacher — remained centered and calm. By trusting the students to want to do right and trusting the circle process to help students regain their self-control, she managed to save the day. Any time a number of students are spinning out of control, you can stop an activity and use this approach to settle students down and try again.

However, there may be some groups of students that are difficult to control in a large circle. If a class is generally disruptive, or if there are a number of students who tend to disrupt a large group activity, you may want to break the group into smaller circles. Put students into small groups of four to six students and give them a go-around question to address among themselves while you walk around the class and monitor what is happening. At the end of the activity, have one student from each group stand up and report back to the whole class what they've discussed. Ideally this method eventually teaches students to work in a large circle as well.

On the Bus

The bus is a continual source of problems in many schools.

Some children spend hours each week on the bus. Often the bus driver is the only adult supervising a busload of children. They would rather worry about negotiating traffic and getting students safely to and from school than deal with behavior problems. When a bus driver does report trouble to the school, it is natural for disciplinarians to think in terms of lecturing and punishing students to attempt to keep them in line. But often a circle is the best way to find out what's going on and get students to take responsibility for their behavior and make changes.

School administrators had to deal with conflict that arose during a shared bus ride between students from an alternative school for at-risk youth, who lived together in a community-based residential group home, and students from a public vocational-technical school. The tech-school students told their assistant principal that the alternative-school students were bullying them, so the assistant principal called the administrator at the alternative school. The latter suggested that a circle with all the students might be the best way to deal with and resolve the bus issues. In the meantime, the alternative-school students were suspended from riding the bus.

The administrator at the alternative school first held circles with her own students. The students said that the other students were teasing them, as well. She said, "Listen, you made things unsafe for that bus. You have to take complete ownership for your part in that. What happened? What were you thinking? If you were mad about them teasing you, what was it you really wanted the kids to hear you say?"

They talked about these issues, and they role-played what it would be like to meet with the other students. The administrator said, "You need to tell them how you felt when they teased you, but you also need to tell them what you did wrong, and that you know you need to make things right. How do you think you can do that? What would you say? How would it look? What kind of help do you need?"

The assistant principal from the public school was familiar with circles, too, and he prepped his students for the meeting. The circle was held at the tech school, with the administrator of the alternative school facilitating. Before the circle, she selected one of her students to go first, because she knew that person would set a good tone for the circle. The group used a small ball as a talking piece. To avoid an "us against them" atmosphere, the facilitator mixed the seating of the kids so students from the two groups would speak alternately. The bus driver and a teacher from the tech school attended the circle, as did a group-home parent who had to drive the students to and from school during their bus suspension. There were 16 people in all.

The circle addressed the prepped questions: "What happened? What was your part in making this bus feel unsafe? What did you say or do, and how did you contribute?" During the first few go-arounds, the alternative-school students spoke more than the tech-school students. But when the tech students saw that the alternative-school kids were taking ownership for their part in the conflict, they too became comfortable speaking up and taking responsibility for how they had contributed to the problems. One of them admitted, for instance, that he'd said something about getting a gun. He said that he would never really do that, but that's how angry and hurt he felt about being bullied.

The facilitator didn't rush the circle. She asked a lot of follow-up questions and gave everyone ample time to speak: "Is there anything else that hasn't been said? What else happened? How do you feel about what's happened? What do you need to do to make things right? What do you need from other people?" Individual students came up with specific plans for themselves.

Toward the end of the circle, the facilitator asked, "How will we know you're following through with all this?" Students said they would check in each morning in school, and they created a bus log for students to sign off on so there would be a written record, too. After the circle, the alternative-school students were allowed to ride the bus again, and no further problems were reported.

There are many important features to this story, including the importance of prepping people in advance of a circle and broadening the circle to include as many of the people affected by an incident as possible. But a major point to take from this anecdote is to remember to *be persistent* when running a circle. On a first go-around, many times people say little or speak superficially. In this example, the alternative-school students were forthcoming from the outset, but it took some time for the tech-school students to see what the circle was about and begin to admit their part in the problems. Sometimes no one really digs in during the first go-around.

When a facilitator allows uncomfortable silences, asks follow-up questions and makes time for multiple go-arounds, people will delve more deeply into an issue. A major breakthrough in this circle happened when the student admitted having said something about wanting to "get a gun." He took a big risk admitting that at a time when many schools have zero-tolerance policies requiring suspension or expulsion when students brings weapons to school. Threats about using weapons are taken seriously and can land a student in deep trouble. However, when the student realized the circle was a safe place to get to the bottom of the problem, he opened up and spoke honestly. His honesty was a successful catalyst toward resolution of the conflict.

In the next example, a circle allowed a bus driver to explain how he felt about students misbehaving on his bus, and the response was instantaneous.

A retired man decided to take a part-time job as a bus driver. He really liked and cared about the alternative-school students he drove, and he made a point of doing nice things, like bringing them donuts and treats. But the students took his kindness for weakness and made a game of the bus ride. They acted crazy, shouted and made noise, ran around the bus, left trash all over the place, threw things out the windows and yelled at people in the streets.

When the school's counselors first learned of the problem, they tried to deal with the students individually. Students met with their counselors, made promises to behave, and wrote and signed behavior contracts that included consequences for not following the rules on the bus, all to no avail. Eventually the school administrator called the bus driver and asked if he would come early to the school one day for a circle.

When the circle convened, the bus driver was the first to speak. He said to the students in the circle, "No one else wanted this bus run because of the types of kids on this bus. But I really like all of you, and I felt I could really make a difference. That's why I brought you stuff and tried to be nice. I took it personally when you left trash behind. The bus company, when I complained, told me to quit this run. But I don't want to do that."

The students were blown away by what they were hearing. The facilitator didn't have to do anything. Immediately a student raised his hand. He said, "I'm really sorry, I didn't know you felt that way. I was one of the idiots doing those things. I promise to change." One by one the students apologized, took responsibility and said what they'd do to support the bus driver. Afterwards, the administrator who facilitated the circle commented, "I wish we had done that circle earlier."

The power of empathy cannot be underestimated. When students had a chance to hear firsthand how that bus driver felt about them, they felt badly, immediately promised to change and followed through. In fact, the students became friends with the bus driver. A week later when a girl brought cupcakes to celebrate her birthday, she made a special point of making an extra cupcake for the bus driver.

In fact, circles often result in the conflicting parties becoming friendly afterward.

> Two boys got into a fight at the bus stop, and one of the boys had his glasses broken. The boys and their families agreed to a circle meeting. The boys not only resolved the problem to everyone's satisfaction, but they started going to each other's houses after school to play video games and became friends.

However, it is also important to be aware of ways in which a circle can go wrong if it isn't prepped correctly. For a serious incident, doing legwork before the circle happens is absolutely essential, as in the first bus incident between the students from the two schools. In the following case, the prep work indicated that some of the participants weren't ready to meet in a circle, but the facilitator ignored the warning signs. The results were uncomfortable and damaging.

> A bus driver complained of student misbehavior on a bus ride. A circle was planned, and the parents of the students involved were invited to attend the circle, along with the students and the bus driver. As soon as the circle began, however, the parents of the misbehaving student started verbally attacking the bus driver for things they believed he had done wrong.

We can recognize this type of defensiveness, "attack others," as a natural response to the shame they felt for their children's actions, as discussed in Chapter 2. Here it resulted in the parents haranguing the bus driver, and the circle had to be aborted.

The facilitator who ran this circle admitted that the participants had not been correctly prepped. She reflected honestly about her mistake, saying, "If people clearly have a bad attitude beforehand, don't do a circle. You can't rush it, even if it takes a few extra days."

The Baggage We Carry

Many conflicts and misbehaviors that manifest during school originate outside the school building. Children come to school with unresolved feelings about things that happened at home and in the neighborhood, involving family and friends, strangers and acquaintances. Punitive responses fail to address the root causes of this behavior. Restorative practices and circles provide a forum for students to talk about what's going on beneath the surface.

For example, a fight broke out during a weekend retreat for teenage boys placed in a drug-and-alcohol-abuse program. The fight turned out to be a symptom of unresolved feelings rather than true conflict between the boys.

> On Father's Day, a group of boys were walking to an Alcoholics Anonymous meeting when a ruckus erupted among several of the boys. Two boys started to fight on the steps of the church where the meeting was being held. Staff intervened and quickly broke up the fight, and the boys continued into the church. Afterward, the counselors got wind of what was really going on. They convened a circle with all the boys and said, "Hey, do you guys need to talk about Father's Day?" One of the two boys who had been in the fight started crying and said, "You know, I really miss my dad."
>
> It turned out that most of the boys had conflicted feelings about their fathers. Those feelings got churned

up by the knowledge that it was Father's Day. The staff decided to ditch all their other plans and focus on questions like "Who is your dad?" and "What do you feel about your father?" Some boys had fathers who were absent or who they didn't even know, and this was painful. Others had conflicts with the fathers they lived with. Eventually the discussion turned to the question of what it would mean to be a good father. By the end of the circle, the boys who had gotten into the fight hugged each other.

Similar issues come up in schools all the time. Too many students come to school worried about broken families, drug and alcohol abuse in the home, violence in their neighborhoods and a host of other serious issues. As funding for sending students to alternative programs gets tighter and tighter, schools recognize the need to find tools for reaching out to their most challenging youth. Some have started their own alternative schools within the school. Because many students do not have the support of their families and communities, schools are forced to take up the slack. Circles provide a forum for students to support one another to deal with these very real problems.

Sometimes teachers worry that they are being asked to be counselors or social workers and solve young people's personal problems. Rather, circles provide a practical forum for the resolution of underlying feelings that intrude into the classroom and disrupt learning. The circle allows young people to express their feelings and, in doing so, reduce their intensity. The circle creates opportunities for students to recognize that others have similar issues and that they are not alone. By expressing feelings and getting acknowledgment from others, most students are then able to put their problems aside and move on with the school day. Hearing about students' problems, teachers may then encourage or arrange for students to meet with a counselor or social worker for more individual assistance.

In the following anecdote, a teacher knew a student was troubled and wanted to help but didn't know what to do. The student requested a circle himself, and then used the circle to talk about his problems. The teacher wrote:

Last year in October, a student's mother was murdered on a Saturday night. I was informed of the situation, but many students had not heard about the incident over the weekend. On Monday morning, to my surprise, the student arrived at school. (Let's call him Jack.) At the beginning of first block, Jack entered the classroom, sat in the back of the room and put his head down. Other students were asking him if he was okay and what was wrong. He didn't answer. The bell rang, and the class began working on their bellwork [a daily student activity at the start of each class]. I walked to the back of the room, placed my hand on Jack's back and asked him if there was anything I could do. He looked up at me, red-eyed from crying, and asked me if we could have a circle. I said absolutely and, as a class, we circled up.

I was very hesitant about how to approach the subject. I wasn't sure how much Jack wanted to talk, so I began the circle by asking the students to do a check-in. We performed this in a "popcorn" [non-sequential circle] format so Jack wouldn't have to speak if he didn't want to. After seven or so students answered, Jack put his hand up for the talking piece. He told his story and even pleaded for the class to always cherish every moment they have with the people they love, to not hold grudges and forgive as best they could. He had gotten into a fight with his mother a few weeks prior to the murder, and since he lived with his father, he hadn't talked to her since. He regretted not resolving their differences and wondered if she knew how much he loved her. Jack had tears in his eyes, and the class was silent.

Then another student asked for the talking piece and said, "Of course she knows how much you love her, and if she didn't, you just told her." Students went around and offered their condolences to Jack, and some asked him why he had come to school. Jack responded by saying, "I had to come. I couldn't sit at home anymore and think about it over and over again. I needed to be with my friends and feel somewhat normal." The students in the class were acting as his counselors. Jack had a great deal of healing to do, and this was by no means the end of his emotional journey, but it was definitely the beginning of his healing process.

If trust had not been established within the class through prior circles, Jack would never have felt comfortable opening up in class. Sometimes performing circles is difficult, but in the end, when it really counts, the payoff is enormous.

Common issues in schools are conflicts between students that originate in the past, at other schools or in the community. Knowing that there are outside circumstances expands the context and assists authorities in resolving issues rather than simply punishing students for their behavior. An alternative school administrator wrote:

We had an incident where a male student smacked a female student. They knew each other from public school and had both been instigating each other. We invited both sets of parents and students and the counselors who worked with them to a circle. The focus of the circle became about safety. The girl's mom told the boy how it really scared her that her daughter could be hit at school. It had a big impact on this boy and his father, who acknowledged this during the circle.

Schools provide a great community service when they

recognize that students' emotional baggage has to be addressed *before* learning can happen. When schools have methods for helping students deal with their issues honestly and openly, they transform the community and make the school a safe haven.

Students in a Canadian alternative school within a public school commented, "If we'd had circles when we were in regular school, things would've been different." They believed that circles at a younger age would have helped them cope with the problems that had made them feel so disconnected at school. Incidentally, the students in this program received training and facilitated their own circles, a practice that has proved quite successful.

Incidents of Hatred

Hurtful acts in schools may sometimes be directed against a racial or ethnic group, or students with a disability. These very hurtful acts have specific victims and also impact a wider community both in and out of the school. While these incidents pack a high emotional charge, circles can be used to bring hard feelings to the surface and allow people to share their voices in a safe setting.

Students at a football game believed they saw opposing visiting team fans raise a confederate flag in the stands. Rumors also flew that visiting players used racial slurs against the home team players and fans. The incident was reported in the press and created a sensation on social media. Both school communities reeled as allegations, denials and arguments ensued. The home team was from a more urban, diverse area, and the visiting team a more rural part of the state. People from each school used these differences as a basis for sustaining stereotypical views of each other.

A dean from the home team school, with responsibility for maintaining positive school culture, was asked by his administration to formulate a restorative response. He chose to create a school culture exchange. Half a dozen students from his more urban school, including football players and student leaders, met with seven students from the rural high school of the opposing team.

The students took tours of each other's schools and ate lunch together. In talking circles, each student shared how they felt about the incident, cleared up misconceptions they had about each other and made commitments about where to go next. The students came away from this experience deeply affected and determined to share their experience throughout their communities.

To ensure that the positive effects of the circles would spread beyond the small groups, after the exchange, each student team spoke at an all-school assembly. Afterwards, the two schools participated in sporting events and other school activities with out incident. The students who were involved in the circles remained in touch and look for other ways to connect with each other.

Since this was a situation where the allegations were unconfirmed and offenders were not known, it made sense to allow a group of caring students to represent each of their schools. The example demonstrates a major contention of this book: talking in an organized setting can help a community heal.

Another incident involved two young adult students in Hungary who were arrested for drawing swastikas and racist symbols on large posters in a public street display. The posters showed large photographs of teenagers with Down syndrome along with inspiring quotations from them, such as, "I accept people for how they are. Do you?" The swastikas would have been incendiary in any setting, but juxtaposed with messages of tolerance from the courageous teens, the defacement seemed all the more hurtful.

Though a criminal case was pending, the two offending students were given an opportunity to sit down with their own families and supporters, as well as the youth and families they denigrated, and hear how everyone was hurt by their defacement of the posters. The offenders admitted they had been using drugs and alcohol when they drew the graffiti. They said they never imagined they could hurt so many people by their thoughtlessness and impulsivity.

At one point, one of the two students, a young woman, was crying. The boy whose quote was used in the poster walked over to her in the middle of the circle. He said – slowly, because speech was challenging for him – "I don't want you to cry because of me," and he hugged her.

The facilitator of the circle was deeply touched by that interaction because it demonstrated "how reconciliation and peace can be done if we allow people to approach each other and feel each other's emotions without defensiveness."

The two students agreed to pay reparations for the damage to the posters. They also agreed to share their story with other students on campus so that they might benefit from their experience.

Be advised that these types of circles require additional care and courage to arrange and conduct. Think through what issues might arise, who are the best people to be present and have preparatory discussions with participants. In the best circumstances, full restoration is possible. This is not always the case, and sometimes bad feelings remain. In our experience, however, the outcome is almost always better than if no circle was held.

Dangerous Situations

Unfortunately, no school today is immune to the potential for devastating violence. One school principal credits restorative practices for creating an environment where students came forth with information that helped abort a potential Columbine-like incident.

A high school student, who was angry with his parents and discontented with his home situation and who had been previously bullied at middle school for being quiet and different, got lost in the crowd during high school and failed ninth grade. In his second year of high school he stole his father's gun and gave it to a friend to hide. The father reported the theft, but the case was not solved. The boy told his friend that he planned to bring the gun to school early one morning, position himself at the top of the busiest stairway, and start shooting at students as they arrived for the day.

Before the student carried out his plan, either he or his friend leaked the plot to other students, who told a teacher what they knew. When confronted, the two students with the gun admitted to the plan, the gun was found and the students were arrested. The principal commented, "Before we started using restorative practices, no one ever talked to 'the man.' But students learned they could trust the school. I always say, 'Relationships are stronger than metal detectors.'"

Because the DA [district attorney/public prosecutor] was investigating the crime, the school did not make a public announcement of the arrest. But several days later when the DA announced indictments, the media arrived with helicopters and news vans and turned the school into a national news circus. Because the media sensationalized the story and made it sound like disaster had just been averted minutes before, parents thought their children were in danger and called the students' cell phones.

The school responded by immediately having teachers

run circles in every classroom. The teachers explained what had happened and that no one was in danger. Students talked to one another about their feelings, and they supported each other. Afterward, teachers said, "We weren't surprised kids didn't need psychological services. We dealt with it right then and there."

The regular use of circles gave teachers a way to directly address a very serious incident. Instead of word spreading haphazardly from person to person, teachers explained to students what had happened. Children immediately discussed their feelings; they knew they were safe and were able to continue with school.

A suburban high school used circles after a tragic incident in which a student actually did bring a gun to school.

A student at a school with 1,000 students entered the school building with a duffel bag containing an assault rifle. He removed the gun and began shooting the walls and the ceiling. The school went into lockdown, meaning students were ushered into classrooms and teachers locked the doors. The boy roamed the halls and said he wasn't going to hurt anyone, but he shook door handles in an attempt to enter some of the classrooms. Everyone in the school was terrified. Police were called, and the boy turned the rifle on himself and killed himself.

Children were immediately dismissed, and the school was closed for students the next day. However, teachers did attend school and found the cafeteria set up with chairs in circles. Teachers talked to one another, answering the following questions, "What happened? What is the impact on you? What do you need to feel safe and be able to move on?"

The next day, students attended school for half a day. Every teacher started his or her class with a circle.

They asked the same questions that had been asked of them the day before. The circle discussion for some groups lasted the entire class. By the fourth and last period of the abbreviated day, many students were saying, "I was really upset at first, but now I just want to get back to school," which suggests that the circles helped students deal with their feelings.

There was a problem in one of the groups, however. An IIRP trainer who was in the building as a gesture of support for the school helped a teacher manage a circle that was going awry. When the circle began, the first two students set a bad tone. First, a boy said, "I don't care, it doesn't affect me." Second to speak was a girl who hammed it up in a phony, superficial way, saying, "I was like, oh, wow! I came in the class and I was like, damn!"

The trainer stopped them and said, "The school asked us to come to assist in running these circles with the understanding that something awful has happened. This circle is meant to seriously address feelings and to see if anyone needs anything or wants to get something off their chest and ask for help. If I were a student sitting in the circle right now, I know I couldn't say what I was really feeling. I don't judge you, but if you want to do this, everyone needs to take this seriously." Some students agreed with the trainer. One boy said, "You know, that kid said something about this to me. I didn't put two and two together. Am I responsible for what he did?" Other students said, "It's not your fault. You couldn't have known what would happen." The circle continued in a more supportive way.

Restorative practices is not a panacea. In this case, the fact that the school routinely used restorative practices did not prevent a disaster; however, when it came time to figure out what to do next and how to help the students and teaching staff cope with the incident, circles helped the school return to normal.

Note, too, that when students failed to take a circle seriously, a redirecting word from the facilitator cut through the silliness and allowed them to benefit from the circle. The trainer noted, "When people start making jokes, you have to intervene and give other kids a chance to say that they need the circle." When students begin to talk to one another in a real way, others become more serious as well. Speaking even more generally, whenever a circle discussion seems to get off track, simply ask participants to stick to the relevant issues. This will always help keep a circle focused on the business at hand and prevent people from getting frustrated with the process.

Circles can also be conducted in situations when legal or punitive sanctions are required. Two incidents in alternative-school programs illustrate this point. An administrator wrote:

> Our former English teacher years back got frustrated with a kid and actually smacked him in class. We obviously had to report this incident to the state child-abuse hotline as well as contact the boy's grandmom, his guardian. We decided that besides whatever action we would take as an employer, we should have a circle. We invited the referral source, the grandmom, the teacher, the student, his counselor and myself. The circle went incredibly well. Everyone shared how they were affected, with true emotion and some tears. The grandmom gave the teacher great feedback about how she was hurt that someone in her position would do that to a child. It gave some closure to a really uncomfortable situation.

Rather than simply fire the teacher and imagine the issue was put to rest, the administrator held a circle. Circles empower victims and give them a forum to face those who have done them wrong. This creates a sense of real justice.

In the following incident, a student was expelled and arrested for being caught with a knife in school.

A New York City alternative school received restorative practices training, and within a few weeks staff felt comfortable running circles. Student leaders began to emerge, too. One of these student leaders was in the hall having a friendly conversation when he stretched his hands in the air. An IIRP trainer happened to notice that he had a huge knife in his pocket. He thought, "Oh, no! This kid is a positive leader, but I can't ignore this."

He told the school principal what he'd seen. A school police officer was also present. The trainer said he hated to see the boy get in trouble, and the principal said he'd wished the trainer had told him outside the policeman's hearing. The student would have to be arrested.

Together they came up with a plan. They called the student to the office and asked the policeman not to put him in handcuffs immediately. The principal said, "Someone saw that you have a knife. Do you?" The boy answered, "Yes." The principal said, "Give it to me." The boy complied, apologized and explained, "I go across half the city to get to school. This knife isn't for school. It's for protection outside."

The principal said, "The police officer knows about this, and you know what is going to happen." The boy said, "Yeah, I know." The principal said, "I want you to have a positive leaving." He offered the boy the chance to go to the class and tell everyone what had happened and why. In the circle, the boy said, "I really screwed up. I want you to know I didn't want to hurt anyone here. This has to do with people who are after me on the outside."

Some students said stuff like, "I would have stashed the knife somewhere." One said, "I hear what you're saying, but I'll walk with you to the subway if that will help you." Another boy, who was a gang leader, said, "Don't start bringing stuff in here. Leave your stuff on the outside. Remember how bad it was here last year? Don't go back to that." Knowing who had incriminated the boy never became an issue. Even the police officer came out of the situation well. The general attitude was, "This is an unfortunate thing that's happened."

It's ironic that no one wanted the boy to be arrested. The circle accepted the unfortunate facts of the situation and gave students a chance to talk to each other and for the student to say goodbye. The student ended up returning to the school eventually. As a way of saying thank you, he installed a speaker system in the cafeteria.

Finally, when something of a serious nature happens in the culture, society or community and disrupts people's normal way of operating, hold a circle. After events like the September 11 attacks or the Columbine shooting, adults and children across the country were shaken. Rather than ignore or gloss over people's feelings, take a break from business as usual and hold circles so students can express their feelings and process what they think about these incidents. Circles have a calming influence in these situations, and for those students who feel too emotional or stirred up to participate, simply permit them to opt out of the discussions.

Deaths

The anecdotes in this chapter demonstrate how broadly circles may be applied, from dealing with minor classroom incidents to serious disruptions of an entire school. In the following example, a small alternative school experienced the tragedy of two staff deaths within a week of one another.

A full-time counselor at an alternative school was killed

early one Friday morning when a train struck the car he was driving. The staff were called, told what had happened and asked to arrive early for a circle in the school's art room. There the school administrator told the staff everything she knew. People asked questions, expressed shock, held hands and chose to pray. Finally, everyone collected themselves and conducted a circle for the entire school of about 40 students.

The staff gave the students what information they had and did a go-around where students expressed their feelings, talked about what they were going through and asked questions. Then they broke into smaller groups where students told stories about the counselor, shared memories and talked about other times they'd experienced grief. Students comforted one another and cried a lot. In the afternoon some students watched a movie while others put together a memorial bulletin board.

After the students went home, the staff sat in a circle and talked, as the students had done. They talked about their workmate, their good memories and their feelings. People expressed anger and denial, as well as sadness and loss. They continually went around the circle, and everyone had a different thought each time around. The staff also held small circles for students the following Monday to see how students were feeling after the weekend and to provide information about the funeral for those who wanted to attend.

When the deceased counselor's mother and sister came to the school to pick up his things, students showed them the memorial board. Later they returned with the father, brother and sister-in-law and donated sports equipment to the school, which they presented to all the students seated in a circle. During a go-around the children shared their good memories of the counselor with his family. The family appreciated the stories the students shared and said they had learned a little more about what their loved one was like at work. They told the students how much he had enjoyed his job.

The following Friday, just as things were getting back to normal, the school's social studies teacher failed to show up for work. The administrator called the man's father, who told him that his son had killed himself. A similar series of circles were held as the week before, but this time, grief and crisis counselors were called to the school to run circles with small groups of students. They said, "We don't know your teacher and counselor. Tell us about what kind of people they were." Many students cried and grieved.

A month later, half a dozen students put together a very unique memorial circle. They turned off the lights and lit candles. People read poems, sang a song and displayed drawings. There was a slide show, and someone read something one of the deceased staff members had written in college. People were given a chance once more to say anything they wanted.

These circles addressed loss without turning away. They were restorative because they helped the groups acknowledge death and look to the future. We have presented these tragic examples so that people have a sense of the circle's full range of potential usefulness.

Why Do Circles Work?

When some people hear anecdotes of children changing their behavior because of something said in a circle, they simply refuse to believe this could happen. Accustomed to authoritarian systems of discipline that perpetuate a feeling of staff versus students, they have trouble acknowledging that another way of working with people is possible.

Circles present a genuine alternative. The circle represents a fundamental change in the relationship between students and authority figures. It creates a cooperative atmosphere in which students take responsibility for their actions. Students respond because they feel respected and realize that what they say matters.

The assistant principal, who at the beginning of this chapter conducted a circle in the out-of-control art room, went on to run many circles in his school. He described a circle in which he perceived a tangible shift in students' attitudes: "I think the turning moment, and I could see it in the students' faces, [was] when they realized they had a say. They realized they were participants, that they were going to be listened to. They could have input."[2]

Even at a very young age, children are able to articulate what is so special about circles. Students at a British primary school said, "Circles are good because everyone gets treated with the same respect," and "I like circles because we can all be taken into account." Others said, "If somebody comes in in the morning and feels sad, if they tell the circle then we'll cheer them up for all the day," and "Circles are good because everybody gets a chance to speak, and even the quiet ones do." Finally, a student commented, "In year five, I used to be real naughty, but the circles changed me ... It makes me feel guilty when I know I've made other people sad" (Cafesociety.org, 2008).

Circles make students feel like partners, and they respond by working to help create a more positive atmosphere. When the light dawns in students' minds and they begin to understand that they are truly being given a stake in their class and school, they rise to the occasion.

Reacting to Something Good That Happened

Responsive circles are not limited to problems. You may also

---

2. To view a video about the use of Restorative Practices at West Philadelphia High School see http://www.iirp.edu/westphilahigh/

react when things go right. A great time to call a circle is when a group of students has had a success or changed a negative pattern of behavior.

A sports team was plagued with physical fights between players. The players participated in a circle to resolve their problems and prevent the fights from occurring. Several weeks later the school counselor who facilitated that circle bought pizza for the group and invited the students to a follow-up circle to celebrate the fact that there had been no more fights.

When things go right, hold a circle. Ask students to discuss what is different in their class or group and what their challenges have been. Have them explain what it feels like in the new class-room environment. Ask if there is anything else they'd like to change about their class or group.

A principal held a circle to express her appreciation for teachers' willingness to adapt to a district initiative that resulted in increased job responsibilities. The circle focused on aspects of the project the teachers were look-ing forward to and invited them to share issues of concern. The circle developed into a brainstorming session to create a support system to advance the project. Teachers reported feeling appreciated, supported and connected as they moved forward.

Reacting to something good that has happened provides two types of constructive feedback. The facilitator, by holding the circle, acknowledges the positive behavior. Beyond that, people have a chance to give feedback to one another. Students feel proud when they make changes, and adults also like to share when they achieve something. These good feelings further reinforce the positive behavior being discussed.

Punishment vs. Making Things Right

Restorative practices makes a crucial distinction between punishment and natural consequences, including making things right or repairing harm. A punishment is meant to inflict some form of suffering on someone who has done something wrong, on the assumption that it will change their behavior. As a rule, punishment is done *to* students.

A natural consequence is a response to wrongdoing that follows logically from what has occurred. Natural consequences work *with* students. When things can be made right, the needs of those who were impacted or harmed by what happened are met. Often no other consequence is necessary.

Students may be engaged to help come up with how to make amends, but consequences may also come from teachers and administrators. The important thing is that students are made to understand why the consequence follows logically from the behavior to which it is a response. Informal responsive circles or small impromptu conversations can be an effective means to make space to explore the impact of hurtful actions and repair the harm. The restorative questions frame the conversation leading up to the final question, "What needs to happen to make things right?" The process allows those who have done the harm and those who were harmed to create a plan of reparation together.

One day, the first two boys to class were greeted at the door by their social studies teacher, who remained in the hallway to greet the other students as they arrived. When the bell rang, the teacher entered the class and asked everyone to get to their warmup, which she had written on the board. That's when she noticed the board had been erased, and the two boys who arrived early were laughing. She asked them if they had erased the work, and they admitted they had.

She immediately circled up the class and asked the boys to explain how they thought their prank impacted her and the rest of the class. They said their actions caused the teacher to have to do extra work and talked about how hard the teacher works, how much she cares about the students and that the "joke wasn't funny."

The teacher asked how the boys could make things right. They said they needed to apologize and they would rewrite the notes on the board for her. She agreed but stated that she needed more. Since they regularly got to class early, she said she would like them to write her class directions on the board for the next few days, to which they agreed. Finally, the boys apologized for their disrespect to the teacher and the time they took from the class. They followed through on their commitment to write up the notes.

The actual form of a punishment and a natural consequence may appear to be the same. A common form of punishment in U.S. schools is known as "detention." Here a student is usually required to stay after school and sit quietly in a room for an hour. But there is often little or no relationship between the actual infraction and this punishment. The detention simply serves as a punishment to inflict discomfort or inconvenience on the assumption that it will change behavior.

However, if a student has consistently failed to complete homework, and the teacher makes them stay after school to complete it and provides the student with assistance, the detention begins to look more like a natural consequence of the student not completing assignments. The difference is the intention of the consequence. Students tend to respond more positively to natural consequences than to punishments, particularly if they are engaged in a constructive process.

A diverse, urban elementary school in Michigan

instituted circles during lunch detention. During this detention, students go to a room separate from other students and aren't allowed to play outside. The school's restorative practices counselor administers the detentions as a restorative process.

Children do circle go-arounds on a range of topics, including thinking about the behaviors that got them into detention in the first place. When the counselor began the new circle format for the detentions, students weren't sure at first what they thought about it. But by the third day the so-called "worst kid" was telling the other students to sit in their seats and respect the circle process.

In fact, students kept coming back for the circle even when they didn't have detention that day, and the restorative practices counselor had to make them go out to recess and play. A parent came to her and said, "We're really glad you're offering this."

Similarly, an urban high school uses circles during after-school detentions. Go-around questions encourage students to talk to one another about what has been happening. Teachers sometimes ask several students who are late to class or not getting to their work right away to meet after school for a problem-solving circle to figure out how they can change their patterns of behavior.

Formal Restorative Conferences

Finally, a word on formal restorative conferences, a specialized type of circle that is generally reserved for reacting to the most serious incidents that happen in a school. The formal conference evolved in the criminal justice field and has been adapted to schools and other settings. What distinguishes the formal conference from other circles is the amount of planning required by the facilitator and the actual structure of the meeting. Conferences usually follow a script — a series of questions that the facilitator asks of all the parties involved in the conference — whereas more flexibility is permitted during a regular circle.

Conferences have been used to address a wide range of problems in schools, including vandalism, fights in and out of school, fire alarms being set off for fun, gang disputes, cursing at teachers, drugs being sold or used in school and feuds outside school between parents of students.

Because conferences bring together victims and offenders, as well as related parties and others affected by an incident, they often include people only indirectly related to the school or bring together students and staff from different schools. The outcomes often rely on the creativity of the participants. For example:

> Some boys from an Australian primary school sold fake raffle tickets to senior citizens. After a conference was held, the offenders paid back the money and performed gardening for an elderly victim as restitution. This restored the relationship between the children and the woman they had wronged, who came to see them as "young boys, instead of hoodlums."[3]

The planning for the restorative conference requires the conference facilitator to meet with all the parties in advance of the conference to explain the structure of the meeting and to ensure that the offender has taken full responsibility for their offense and will not re-victimize the people they have already hurt. The facilitator answers any questions the participants have, anticipates any special needs and arranges a place to hold the conference, which may be a public or neutral venue other than the school. Conference facilitators usually also arrange for the participants to share some snacks or refreshments after the formal conference is over,

---

3. Quoted from "Restorative Practices at Queanbeyan South, an Australian Primary School," by Abbey Porter, Restorative Practices eForum, April 19, 2005.

which provides informal meeting time for participants to talk in a friendly way. Incidentally, the facilitator need not be an employee of a school, but may be a neutral party, such as a police officer or community volunteer trained in the restorative conferencing process.

See the IIRP and the Piper's Press *Restorative Justice Conferencing: Real Justice and the Conferencing Handbook*, two books in one volume, which provide a wealth of stories and a comprehensive procedural explanation of the formal restorative conference — the most structured form of responsive circle.

CHAPTER 5

Staff Circles

One of the most frequently overlooked applications of circles is their use among teachers and professional staff. Just as with students, circles are effective for engaging everyone in a group in decisions and discussion, allowing quiet voices to be heard and dealing with problems and conflict.

The IIRP did a training of teachers in an elementary school in a major U.S. city. One of the questions raised during a circle discussion was "Are there any major obstacles to employing restorative practices here?" A number of teachers pointed out that the school didn't have staff meetings. The principal said that there was no time during the day to hold teachers' meetings. The teachers argued they needed to build trust among one another to make restorative practices work throughout the school. They said they didn't even know everyone's first names.

The principal turned the problem right back over to her staff. She reiterated the problem and asked what could be done. In the circle, teachers repeated that they'd like to get to know each other better and that they hoped they could find a time to meet. Some teachers said they were meeting informally in the library every day for ten minutes before the school day started. They said everyone could meet together then, see each other's faces and share a story or two. The meetings were implemented the next day.

Because this was a group idea, rather than a suggestion of the principal's, there was immediate buy-in from most of the staff. Just as teachers and administrators who do things *with* students, rather than *to* them or *for* them, build relationships and give students the opportunity to take responsibility for their actions and the results, administrators who work *with* those they supervise build good rapport with employees.

Circles with staff may be used proactively, as in the first example, or responsively, as in the following case:

The IIRP was hired by a well-regarded U.S. school district to hold a circle with the teachers of its English department. There wasn't any strife within the department, but the administration was convinced that the teachers in the department were not acting as a team.

During the first go-around with the teachers, the conversation was rather surface and superficial. Teachers mainly talked about how they liked the school and the district.

On the second go-around, one teacher went deeper. First he said he was proud to be a teacher in the school and that he had in fact taken a job there because of the school's good reputation. He acknowledged that his colleagues were some of the best educators with whom he had ever worked. But then he said, "Honestly, I feel like I'm on an all-star team." He paused and then continued, "But you know what? I never watch all-star games, because everyone's out for themselves, and no one puts the team first."

This risky statement had the effect of changing the entire tenor of the conversation. Teachers began to identify that there was an underlying tone of competition rather than collaboration within the department. During the circle, teachers affirmed their mutual high regard for one another. They identified a need to have a way to get to one another to talk about concerns and problems. This was something they felt they had never been invited to do. In the final go-round everyone made a commitment to explore ways to act differently to increase trust and communication between members of the department.

As with circles for youth, circles with adults may take one of any number of formats, depending on the needs, requirements and differences of various schools. Some examples include:

> Regular staff meetings
> Department meetings
> Special meetings for the delivery of information and the solicitation of staff response and feedback
> Problem solving
> Professional development
> In-service meetings
> Fostering communication within and between departments
> Meetings among administrators in a school
> Meetings among principals at various sites in a district
> Supervision
> Goodbye circles when someone leaves or moves to another job within a school or district

Using Circles to Learn About Circles

One of the best ways for schools to facilitate the implementation of circles is by holding regular circle meetings with staff. These meetings should focus on how teachers are using circles and what they are doing to be restorative in the classroom. Experience is the best teacher. When teachers share their experiences in an open forum, ideas for things to try in the classroom spread rapidly.

A video used in IIRP trainings shows how an administrator successfully created a circle for teachers to talk with one another in a real way about things they were doing in their classrooms. One teacher talked about how in his Spanish class he was brusque with a girl who was misbehaving and had let her grades slip. Later he made a point of talking with her and engaging her restoratively, and together they came up with ways for her to do better in class. Another teacher talked about a student who was challenging to her and how she finally won him over. A third teacher discussed how she worked with students to get them to be more helpful in the art classroom and put clay away properly.

The specifics of the stories are interesting, but, more important, in the video you can see the trust and respect these teachers had for one another in the circle. They were willing to admit their challenges and discuss how they were working to improve their classrooms and develop different ways of working with students. Often in a professional setting people believe they must act like they have all the answers, but in the circle shown in the video people made themselves vulnerable, removing the barriers between them. The circle allowed them to learn from and encourage each other.

A circle about circles should be conducted on a regular basis when a school initiates the use of circles. If teachers meet every four weeks to talk about what they've tried doing with circles, it goes a long way toward building trust and relationships among teachers. When teaching staff experience circles themselves, they understand how it feels for children to sit in circles. Many new ideas result from the sharing of experience, and the circle provides a forum for teachers to support one another.

In the following example, a relevant circle discussion with a group of teachers who were very resistant to the idea of using circles with students demonstrated the power of circles to the teachers. By participating in a real circle, the teachers learned what circles could do for their students.

During the morning session of an IIRP training, the two IIRP trainers got a strange feeling from the reaction of middle-school teachers, who were just back from summer vacation. During a break, the trainers asked each other what was going on. Then the principal said to them, "Look, I should have told you this before. Over the summer we lost two students, and a faculty member died. He probably committed suicide." The two trainers consulted with the principal further, and they agreed to address these issues rather than continue with the standard training activity.

After the break, one of the trainers said to the group, "I heard that some terrible things have happened over the summer. I'm not here to do therapy. But we'd like to try some circles where you can talk about these things. Do some go-arounds, and talk about how you feel about what has happened. Talk about anything you need."

The two teachers who had been most resistant to the training so far that day were big, tough-looking guys. They were seated a quarter of the way around the circle, and both of them began to cry during their turns to speak. One said how close he had been to the man who died and how sad he was about the death.

People wondered aloud how they should talk to the students about what had happened. They didn't know if they should say that the teacher had killed himself or not. During the circles, they dealt with their feelings and made a plan for ways to talk with students.

After this emotional circle, the vast majority of the teachers said they hadn't really understood what the circles were about until they'd had a chance to see for themselves what a circle could do. Now they understood why this would be valuable for children.

Staff Meetings Using Circles

When teachers are seated in a circle during a meeting, there are opportunities throughout the meeting for people to respond to information that is presented. A check-in at the start of a meeting may be used to gauge how teachers are feeling, to report on good news and to get feedback about problems people may be having. Teachers may share personal as well as professional information, particularly if the intention is to build rapport and help staff get to know one another better. The feedback provides administrators with information and helps teachers feel more comfortable talking to one another.

An entire meeting need not be conducted in a circle format for circles to play a part. Rather, the meeting may be largely administrator-centered and the circle format used only when responses are sought. For instance, an administrator might ask teachers to respond with their thoughts on how to successfully implement a new procedure. At the next meeting the administrator might ask, "What's working and what's not working, and how might we make improvements?" Other possible questions include:

> How is everyone doing with the new protocols for grading?
> How are things going in the cafeteria or at recess?
> Have things improved on the buses?
> How are people feeling about the new scheduling system/ parking rules/[fill in the blank]?

As with youth, circles may either take the form of structured sequential go-arounds or open non-sequential circles for people to talk about various issues in the school. Asking for feedback and engaging teachers in dialogue may already be a norm, but when it's done in a circle format there is a better chance that more voices will be heard. Just as some students are more reserved than others, some adults are reluctant to speak in a meeting. The circle encourages those people to say something.

When certain people are monopolizing a discussion, and it seems those quiet voices are not being heard or that people have some feelings that aren't being expressed, do a go-around to get a sense of what everyone thinks, and then return to the normal structure of the meeting. Naturally, if people get off topic in a circle discussion, the facilitator should simply remind the group of the focus and bring the discussion back on point.

At the end of a meeting, you might conduct a check-out go-around as a wrap-up. Possible questions include:

> Is there anything you'd like to see addressed in a future meeting?
> What's one thing that you learned from this meeting?
> What can you take from this meeting into the classroom tomorrow?

The following example demonstrates how opening and closing a meeting with a circle go-around gave people both the opportunity to get to know one another better and to resolve conflicts that arose during the meeting.

An all-day meeting of the new board of governors of a new school in England, which would be run on restorative principles, began with circle go-arounds. Fifteen people, only some of whom knew each other, began the day by stating their names and occupational roles and then in three successive go-rounds responded to the following:

1. Tell something fun or funny that happened to you or that you experienced in the last week.
2. What is your expectation of what we're going to do during this all-day meeting?
3. How much do you know about restorative practices? How knowledgeable do you feel?

The first question, which seems the most frivolous, actually turned out to be a great icebreaker. During the first break in the meeting, people approached each other and asked one another about things they'd said. For instance, someone said during the circle that they'd just returned from a vacation to India, and another approached him at the break and said he'd been there, too. A number of informal conversations began with the personal information learned in that first go-round.

Later in the meeting, the discussion became heated at times. People expressed conflicting views and at times challenged one another's ideas. It was a productive discussion, but complicated, and at times people seemed frustrated with one another. After a while, the chairperson of the meeting stopped the discussion and said, "Okay, we've had a rather vigorous discussion. Let's do a go-around and talk about what you think about what's been said so far."

One participant commented afterwards, "It's amazing how this helped people center and get clear on where they stood. People heard different voices, and the quiet voices gave a very centering perspective." Another person noted that the closing check-out go-round allowed people to tidy things up. One person apologized for being angry with someone else in a heated moment. Rather than having people leave with awkward feelings, everyone left feeling that all had been resolved.

Department meetings may be conducted in circles, too. One high school incorporates circles into its "professional learning communities" or PLCs, a concept that fosters collaboration, mutual support and shared responsibility for academic success in schools. During these circle meetings people discuss ways they can work together to increase student performance and test scores.

A youth-services organization uses a similar process, which it refers to as "intravision." During supervision, an administrator provides feedback on performance. Then teachers and other staff bring up their own professional goals and challenges and openly discuss their own approaches and progress. The executive director of the organization noted that everyone in the organization can at any time explicitly state what aspects of their professional selves they are working on. One person may be working on accepting the ambiguity of various work situations, another on drawing clear boundaries with youth, and yet another on following through and communicating clearly and directly with colleagues serving youth in different departments. Since no one is perfect, everyone is comfortable sharing their strengths and being open about the areas in which they need to grow.

The restorative problem-solving fishbowl discussed earlier is also used by this organization to facilitate professional development during larger meetings. One way this is done is for a volunteer to present a problem they are working on. Most of the people present will be seated in the outer circle. The presenter sits in an inner circle with six to ten interested people plus an empty chair. The volunteer presents their situation for about five to ten minutes with no interruptions. The people in the center may then ask a brief clarifying question or two, but otherwise they are limited to making suggestions in the next phase. People often start by phrasing their suggestions as questions, until they are directed to turn them into statements.

After the presentation of the problem, for the next 10 to 20 minutes (the times are adjusted to suit the time constraints of the meeting), people in the inner circle and anyone who wants to occupy the empty seat offer feedback, which generally take simple declarative forms like: "Try using ..." or "Have the student ..." or "Ask the student to ..." Pauses for silence are permitted; these are usually the times when people from the outside circle move to the empty chair in the middle and then return to their seat. Finally, the person with the problem takes a moment to absorb all the ideas, which either they or another person have written down, and comments, without judgment, on one or two things from the list they plan to try out.

Conflicts with Teachers

It's not just students who get in trouble. Staff and teachers also behave in inappropriate ways at times. Principals may respond punitively with strict disciplinary action, but there is also a place for the restorative process.

At a public high school an assistant principal questioned a teacher about how she had handled an incident involving an altercation between a boy and a girl, which ended with the boy bear-hugging the girl and turning her upside down. No one was hurt during the incident. The teacher, however, felt she was being attacked by the assistant principal for her response to the situation, and she walked out of the room while being questioned.

The principal of the school might have taken immediate disciplinary action against the teacher, but instead he chose to respond restoratively. He spoke with the teacher and the assistant principal separately and then decided to bring them together to talk. The teacher admitted that the incident had made her emotionally distraught. She apologized for how she responded to the assistant principal and said she knew she had done the wrong thing and shouldn't have walked out of the room. The assistant principal said he knew that wasn't the way she normally acted. He accepted her apology and said he wanted to move on.

This was a small meeting of just three people, but it took the form of a circle and served to resolve the issue. The principal who relayed this story said he uses this process about eight or nine times per school year when conflicts arise between staff. In another example, the conflict took place over email:

Two teachers argued over which of their departments would pay for an expense. The first teacher wrote, "Your department paid for this last year. Will your department pay for it again?" The second wrote back saying, "No, you're wrong. We didn't pay for this last year, and we won't do it this year, either." The exchange became personal and was broadcast to about 10 people on an in-house email list. When the principal found out, he told the teachers to stop emailing each other and called them into his office. They were so angry with one another the principal made them use a talking piece to stop them from interrupting each other.

The principal said he valued both of the men as staff members, but they needed to resolve the issue. When the teachers finally got past the personal attacks, it became clear they were both right and both wrong. The departments would have to share in the expense, but neither could be responsible for the entire amount.

The principal said the outcome of the meeting was positive: "They were never the best of friends, but they were able to work together after that. And I didn't have to issue any formal reprimands." The principal said he didn't require the teachers to apologize to the other staff who received the emails, but he did ask them to talk to those teachers and explain that the angry exchange should not have happened. The two teachers promised that this would not happen again, and it didn't.

The principal noted that one of the teachers really took the restorative process to heart after the meeting. He describes that teacher as "one of my closest and most trusted colleagues." This is another example that shows when people experience the restorative process themselves, they understand it in a fundamental way and may extend it further in their work.

When a principal or other administrator facilitates a circle in a class, the effect is often beneficial to the teacher as well as students. In a sense, this is another type of staff circle. Numerous examples have been cited in this book that demonstrate teachers taking some responsibility for problems in a class and cooperating with students to make improvements. In a case where a teacher has actually wronged a student, a circle may also be facilitated to process what has happened.

A white teacher accused a black student of a crime of vandalism in front of a class. When the student heard about this, she was very hurt and offended. The principal and assistant principal spoke to the teacher, and the teacher realized what a mistake he'd made by saying things publicly rather than speaking to the student privately. He recognized the trouble this action could cause him professionally. It turned out that the accusation was false. The teacher saw the damage that he'd caused.

Seeing that the teacher was taking ownership of his mistake, the principals suggested a circle meeting be held with the teacher, the student and the student's parents. During the meeting, the student talked about how hurtful this false accusation was to her. While she'd gotten in trouble in the past, she had been trying hard to stay on the straight and narrow. This accusation struck her as a blow to her reputation. The teacher told the student and her parents he realized he had erred, and he apologized. He said, "I messed up. I should not have said that. It was wrong."

Because the teacher was white and the student was black, there was some concern that the parents and student might claim the teacher's accusation was racially motivated. Instead, everyone recognized that the teacher had taken responsibility for his actions and sincerely wanted to restore the relationship. At the end of the meeting, everyone agreed to let bygones be bygones. When the student entered the class the next day, the teacher made a public apology, and the student finished the course and graduated. No other actions were taken, and no other problems resulted.

Toxic Environments

Once a school has spiraled out of control, it may seem impossible to get it back on track. Here's where an outside party running a circle can make a big difference. In the following instances, the IIRP ran circles that allowed people in conflict to see that they also had common interests. In the first case, not everyone's mind was changed, but the circle did clarify for all the participants that it was only a small minority of teachers who were determined to maintain a toxic tone in the school.

An elementary school seemed to be falling apart. People were going over the head of the principal of the school to complain to the assistant superintendent of the district about perceived wrongs that had occurred months and even years before. A circle was convened with all the teachers of the school. After a brief introduction, an IIRP trainer conducted three go-arounds:

First: "Tell about something positive that happened with a student in the past week." This question was meant to set a positive tone and remind people of the common purpose of the teaching staff.

Second: "What are the main issues for us being here today, and what is one thing you've done to maintain this as a problem?" Many teachers responded that the atmosphere in the school was so toxic that they just hid in their classrooms and avoided people.

Third: "What commitment will you make to help make changes, not just tomorrow, but also for the long term?" Some people said, "I'll try to be more direct in communication with other people." Others said, "I know there are people I could be friendly with. I'll try to give them a chance."

If the principal had been running the circle, it is unlikely teachers would have opened up. During the course of the circle, it also became apparent that a few ringleaders were perpetuating the hideous tone. These few people refused to participate. All they would say was, "I can't do anything differently. I do everything fine." On one of the go-arounds one of the worst offenders cried and said, "I just feel like this process makes light of the harm that has been done."

The facilitator immediately confronted this. He said, "I started by saying we couldn't fix this in a day. But I said if you do nothing today, nothing will be different tomorrow." Because he challenged her directly, other teachers who wanted to see things turn around felt emboldened to be positive. It was clear by the end of the meeting that while there were about five vocal leaders who wanted to maintain the acrimonious tone in the school, in fact those people represented a small minority of the teaching staff.

By bringing issues into the open, everyone was able to get some perspective. And the positive voices were no longer crowded out by the loud negative voices.

In another case, the IIRP ran a training for a large urban school with a history of serious problems. Three students had been murdered outside of school as a reaction to fights that had taken place within the school. The reputation of the school in the community was very poor, and many teachers had internalized the negative view of the school and the students. The circle process permitted suppressed voices to be heard, and an alternative view began to emerge:

During a restorative practices training, teachers at a high school were asked to role-play students, but some of the teachers really lost control. Saying they were acting like students, they shouted out, threatened and pushed one another and prevented anyone else from talking.

The trainer stopped the role play, quieted everyone, got everyone into a circle, dropped his head and said, "Is this what your classrooms are like every day?" A few people shouted, "Yeah, that's the way things are!" The trainer replied, "Every student? Every student acts this way? Is this the way it really is?"

Finally someone said, "No, it isn't." There was silence for a moment. The person continued: "That's not the way the majority of our students act. Yes, we have some students that will act that way and take up our time. But I don't like that people are trying to say that that's the way it always is here."

Other people chimed in and said: "Yeah, I'm tired of all the bad press about this school and all the negative things. If we're going to change this, we're going to have to stop buying into this bad image ourselves."

A distinguished-looking gentleman spoke next. He said, "I'm new here. I've only been here two weeks. I have been to almost every other school in this district. I have heard what they say about the students here. Not only are those things not true, but you have students here who are very, very talented."

The teaching staff put forth viewpoints during that circle that challenged the accepted view of the school. The trainer could never have successfully challenged those views himself. But by allowing the circle process to proceed among the teachers and by opening the floor to suppressed voices, he cleared the way for a new type of conversation to take place.

Schools with Residential Facilities

Schools come in many shapes and sizes — private, public and charter, residential and day, small, medium and large. Circles can be adapted for use with staff in all these environments. As an illustration of how this can be done, take the example of a residential school for at-risk youth. Here, administrators use circles to facilitate communication between academic, residential and counseling staff. Every meeting begins with a check-in. Possible go-around questions include:

> How have you been a teammate this week?
> Talk about a child you made a connection with recently.
> What is your spirit or mood today?

The team that is brought together during any given meeting may vary from as few as three to as many as 35 people. The goal is always to foster a shared understanding of how to best serve the children in the organization's care, raise people's awareness of relevant issues and help people understand how and when changes must occur. When problems arise, people often apologize for mistakes and discuss what needs to be corrected. During the circles people also discuss their successes and strive to build on what is working well.

Recently, the residential facility was faced with the prospect of budget cuts. Staff were brought in to be informed of the situation. But they were also engaged in a problem-solving process to come up with ways to cut expenses without having to cut staff or services. In the circles that followed, staff came up with solutions for cutting recreational expenses by looking for free things to do with students. They also came up with a plan for reducing the number of shifts from 130 to 50 by making some scheduling changes, which had the added benefit of creating more continuity for staff members who supervised certain groups of students. While the problem was serious, people felt good about helping to come up with solutions. A follow-up meeting six weeks later showed that in fact there were significant monetary savings.

Unintended Consequences

When positive staff communication resulting from circles becomes commonplace, outcomes may include good results along unexpected lines.

A public school in its second year of implementation of restorative practices wanted to go further, but there was a perception that several teachers, all near retirement age, were being resistant to the changes. As a group, these teachers set a negative tone, which made other teachers uncomfortable and thwarted the development of a more positive atmosphere in the school.

All this came out during a teachers' circle meeting to discuss restorative practices. Some teachers said they hated to go into the faculty room because the older teachers made them feel out of place. As a result of this meeting, the teachers agreed that they would speak up in the faculty room and express how they felt about the negative views of the older teachers. The upshot was that the older teachers vacated and took their lunch breaks in their own classrooms. The more positive teachers took over the faculty room.

What might not have come to light in a management-directed meeting did get brought up in a staff circle, with favorable consequences. A preferred consequence might have been for the older faculty to open themselves to go along with the changes the younger teachers wanted to see, but people cannot be forced to change.

Circles with Administrators

In a very large and sprawling Canadian school district, a

superintendent for the 48 principals in her area of the district ran a spontaneous circle based on an unanticipated situation. The success of that impromptu circle influenced the superintendent to continue using circles with principals on a regular basis. She wrote:

> Every month our system had a principals' meeting where all 104 principals came together. However, one particular month the agenda consisted of person after person getting up to tell the principals what they were not doing and how they had to change. Someone from HR got up and lectured them about hiring procedures and electronically filing personnel changes. Someone from finance got up to lecture them about budget management and budget reports. Next it was someone from the curriculum department lecturing them on holding teachers accountable for instructional practice and the importance of getting their provincial assessment scores up higher.
>
> It was a deadly meeting, and the principals were totally demoralized as they left that afternoon. They all felt that they had been given a "class detention" for the whole day, and no one had commented on all of the hard work they were putting in week after week. Now no one from the board office meant to have this effect on the principals. From their perspective, they were trying to give the principals important feedback so they wouldn't get themselves into hot water, but the principals sure didn't see it that way.
>
> Two weeks later, it was time for my superintendency meeting, and as I watched the principals come into the room, I realized that they were still feeling demoralized. I had never seen that group look so down and dejected. I had a full agenda and as always was concerned about getting through it, since our meetings were only half days. However, as I watched the principals' body language, I

thought, "I can't just launch into my agenda. I have to address this somehow." I spoke to one of the people who worked out of my office and said, "I've got to do something different today — look at them." So we bounced around the idea of doing a circle.

I called aside a couple of the principals and told them what I was thinking of doing. They were supportive, so I said I'd use the questions we use when someone has been harmed. I asked, "If you are okay with it, would you be willing to sit on my right and be the first two principals to respond to the questions?" They agreed, so I asked the principals to move the tables out of the way and to put their chairs in a circle. You could see that some of them were somewhat apprehensive, but they complied.

I started with the two principals on my right, and I asked them, "What did you think at the time [of the principals' meeting]? What have you thought about since? What has been the hardest thing for you? What do you need to have happen to address your needs?"

I was apprehensive as to whether I was doing the right thing; however, I was completely blown away by the responses of the principals. One after another, they spoke with such candor and heartfelt emotion (many of them were in tears as they spoke), but they all wanted to share how they felt and how it was impacting them and their families. After an hour we had done less than a third of the group, so I asked the principals if they wanted to continue. The response was an overwhelming "YES!"

It took the whole meeting to allow everyone to speak and then to discuss what we could do as a group to address their needs in a go-forward fashion. Needless to say, I didn't get to anything on my prepared agenda; however, the outcome of that meeting was incredible. All of the principals spoke about how liberating an experience it was

— how much it helped them to hear from others that they were feeling the same emotions — and how it helped them put things into perspective.

One of the powerful benefits of doing this exercise was how it bonded us together as a group. I received emails and phone calls for days expressing gratitude for doing the circle and giving them a chance to be heard and to listen. News of the meeting spread around the system and principals from other areas of the board came up to me throughout the next couple of months and talked to me about how impressed they were with the word-of-mouth about how effective that "principal circle" had been.

After that success, the superintendent frequently ran those meetings in circles. While subsequently working in another school district, she took the process to principals' meetings there, as well.

The superintendent said she also used the circle process within schools to mediate disputes that would "sometimes crop up between a principal and their staff," not unlike the situation in the elementary school where people were going over the head of the principal and creating a toxic environment in the school. She wrote of this circle process:

> It gave everyone a chance to hear from the administrative as well as the teacher perspective regarding issues that were causing strain on the principal/staff relationship. This was far more effective than having individual teachers filing grievances and having investigations to see who was at fault and whose knuckles needed to be rapped.

One of the fundamental lessons here is the extent to which one must learn to trust the circle process and the ability of people to work through conflict. It seems that no matter the problem, more often than not, people in circles are able to work through difficult issues by talking and listening to one another.

When asked about circles that have gone wrong, the executive director of a nonprofit agency that uses circles extensively with students and staff commented, "Truthfully, not that many have gone wrong. Sometimes people think a circle is bad when there's a lot of emotion. To me, coming from the counseling side of things, it's actually a good thing when people are sharing and being honest about how they feel. Sometimes it's hard for people to hear those things, but it's actually a good thing."

Community Circles and Other Possibilities

Besides schools, circles have been used in social services, prisons, workplaces and the community. Circle facilitators include administrators, police officers, corrections workers and activists. The potential of circles to foster new forms of civic life — to resolve problems and create community connections — is in the early stages.

Here's what resulted when the administrator of an alternative school that employed restorative practices became aware of a problem of unruly behavior, vandalism and graffiti by youth in the community where the school was located. While the problem wasn't thought to be connected to the students of the school, the school was affected by the vandalism and littering, and the problem was taking up a lot of the administrator's time. He decided to be proactive and apply the idea of circles to the community problem:

> The administrator invited neighbors, business owners, police officers and some of the school's students to attend a circle meeting one evening in the school. Through a series of go-arounds, people discussed what harm had been done, how people were impacted and what people would need to have happen in order to make things right again. Everyone said how they were affected by "the youths' bullying,

loitering and property destruction. They were roaming the streets at night, shouting profanities and racial slurs, playing loud music, spray painting buildings and damaging cars."

A police officer who was present urged the group to call the police every time they witnessed something happening or the consequences afterward, because the police would direct more cars to the area based on the calls they received. In fact, neighbors did call and the neighborhood was added to the police department's "hot sheet."

Other outcomes included neighbors talking about developing their own town watch and compiling an email list so neighbors and local businesses could stay in touch more easily. The meeting fostered a new sense of community and inspired people with the feeling that they had the ability together to make a difference. (Welden, 2007)

In contrast to adversarial meetings, circles provide a cooperative forum. People are encouraged and given the opportunity to express their own views, yet circles seek to find common ground between people.

One might imagine what would happen in the future if school boards or town and city governments conducted their meetings, or parts of their meetings, in a circle format. What forms of community involvement and democratic problem solving would become possible if members of the community were invited to have their voices heard in such circles? The implications of circles for participatory democracy have only begun to be explored.

Afterword

Circles are as old as the hills. Human beings' earliest discussions were held by our indigenous ancestors in circles around the fire. Somewhere along the way, as our numbers grew and our social organizations became more complex, we moved out of egalitarian circles into hierarchical structures. Now, often from a raised platform, leaders typically face others seated in rows, with most of the group looking at the backs of the people in front of them.

Yet, in a variety of settings and for a variety of purposes, we are rediscovering the power of circles. For all our technological advances, we have come to realize that we lost something along the way — a very simple and effective technology that fosters mutual understanding and healing in a way that often seems magical.

In circles, we face each other and speak respectfully, one person at a time, diminishing the feeling of disconnectedness that permeates our modern world and restoring the sense of belonging that constitutes healthy human community. We may find this ancient form of social discourse helps us address our greatest challenges.

References

Cafesociety.org (Producer). (2008). *Building our community: A film about restorative practices* [DVD]. Hull, England: Hull Centre for Restorative Practices.

Kim, W. C., & Mauborgne, R. (2013, January). Fair process: Managing in the knowledge economy. *Harvard Business Review, 81*(1), 127-136.

Nathanson, D. L. (1992). *Shame and pride: Affect, sex and the birth of the self.* New York, NY: W. W. Norton.

Nathanson, D. L. (1995). Crime and nourishment: Sometimes the tried and true becomes the tired and false. *Bulletin of the Tomkins Institute, 2,* 25-30.

Nathanson, D. L. (1997). Affect theory and the compass of shame. In M. R. Lansky & A. P. Morrison (Eds.), *The widening scope of shame* (pp. 339-354). New York, NY: Psychology Press.

Pranis, K., Stuart, N., & Wedge, M. (2003). *Peacemaking circles: From crime to community.* St. Paul, MN: Living Justice Press.

Tomkins, S. S. (1962). *Affect imagery consciousness: Vol. I. The positive affects.* New York, NY: Springer.

Tomkins, S. S. (1963). *Affect imagery consciousness: Vol. II. The negative affects.* New York, NY: Springer.

Tomkins, S. S. (1991). *Affect imagery consciousness: Vol. III. The negative affects: Anger and fear.* New York, NY: Springer.

Wachtel, T., O'Connell, T., & Wachtel, B. (2010). *Restorative justice conferencing: Real justice and the conferencing handbook.*

References

Pipersville, PA: Piper's Press.

Webb, D. (2010, January 7). My classroom's journey with restorative practices. *eForum Archive.* Retrieved from https://www.iirp.edu/eforum-archive/my-classroom-s-journey-with-restorative-pracitces

Welden, L. (2007, November 7). A restorative community circle. *eForum Archive.* Retrieved from https://www.iirp.edu/eforum-archive/a-restorative-community-circle

Appendix:
"Using Circles Effectively" Documents

These materials accompany the IIRP's professional development course, "Using Circles Effectively."

Critical Issues in Using Circles

Circles can be related to course content or interpersonal.

Circles help people take responsibility.

Circles allow quiet voices to be heard.

Circles allow leaders to emerge.

Many people will say, "I don't know" or, "Can I pass?" Make sure you have responses to these statements ready.

The shape of the circle is important.

Clear directions increase the likelihood of success.

Leaders should model appropriate participation.

Circles can help people explore issues on a deeper level.

Circles allow people to learn about each other and build relationships.

Circles encourage problem solving.

Using Circles to Respond to Incidents

When an incident occurs that affects a group of students or an entire class, a circle go-around is an effective tool for engaging the students in a discussion to resolve the issue. While not required, it is preferable for the students to already have experienced lower-risk circles. It is sometimes helpful to have any identified "offenders" make some preliminary statements accepting responsibility.

The circle should be used to address two critical questions:
1. What harm has been caused?
2. What needs to happen to make things right?

Older students may simply be able to answer these questions but for many students, particularly in lower grades, the following questions may be helpful:
> What have you thought about since the incident?
> How do you feel about what happened?
> What has been the hardest part of this for you?
> Who has been affected by this incident?
> How have they been affected?
> How did your parents react when they heard what happened?
> What was your part in the problem?
> What needs to happen to make things right?
> What can we do to make sure this doesn't happen again?
> How have you felt in the past when you were teased [or whatever the incident was]?

If the circle has one or two identified offenders, be sure to praise them publicly for their courage in dealing with the incident in such a public way. Always look for ways to reintegrate them and allow them to reclaim their good name in the class.

Getting Started with Circles

Circle go-arounds are a great way to foster a sense of community among students. Also, they allow quieter voices to be heard and limit the amount of time that more talkative students have the floor. Arrange chairs in a circle (younger students may prefer to sit on the floor) and have students answer the question in turn. Frequently, a "talking piece" helps students wait their turn and gives a physical reminder of who has permission to speak. These go-arounds can be used during a separate circle time, as an opening ritual for class discussions or as a tool to process a problem in class. Use one of the following questions or create your own. Remember to start with low-risk questions until students get used to the format. Teachers should always answer the questions, too. Have fun!

> Say something nice about the person to your right.
> What makes you sad (happy)?
> What is your favorite food?
> What is your favorite color?
> What is your favorite TV show?
> If I could be any animal, I would be…
> What makes a good friend?
> Tell about a favorite vacation.
> Tell something fun you did last weekend.
> What is your favorite thing to do?
> What do you do well?
> Why should people follow the rules?

> How do you feel when someone laughs at you?
> Name someone in this class who helped you this week.
> What do you want to be when you grow up?
> I like summer because...
> What is your favorite room in your house?
> Whom do you trust?
> What do you like about this class (or school)?
> What is something you know how to do that you didn't know how to do last year?
> What other student worked hard today?

Remember to praise students for their participation — even if they struggle. Resistance (silliness, refusing to talk, interrupting and so forth) is usually a result of fear and will go away quickly if it is dealt with immediately in a firm but caring way.

"Conflict is inevitable, but my knowledge of how to handle it allows me to restore relationships."

— Lisa Cofield,
   IIRP Graduate, 2011

Maximize Your Ability to Lead Change

The International Institute for Restorative Practices (IIRP) is a graduate institution designed for the 21st century, where learning centers on real-life challenges and projects.

Our students exhibit a pioneering spirit, and together we are fostering restorative practices as an emerging social science.

Learn about our Transparent Tuition and Interest-Free Payment Plan.

International Institute
for Restorative Practices

www.iirp.edu
610-807-9221

About the IIRP

All humans are hardwired to connect. Just as we need food, shelter and clothing, human beings also need strong and meaningful relationships to thrive.

Restorative practices is an emerging social science that studies how to strengthen relationships between individuals as well as social connections within communities.

The IIRP Graduate School is the first graduate school wholly dedicated to restorative practices.

IIRP faculty are the world's leading experts in the ideas and competencies they teach. They help their students tailor their studies and facilitate meaningful online engagement with fellow students from around the world. Courses are online, allowing students to study where they live and work.

Based in Bethlehem, Pennsylvania, USA, the IIRP has trained over 100,000 people in 85 countries. Along with our affiliates, partners and licensed trainers in the United States, Canada, Europe, Latin America, Africa, Asia and Australia, we are fostering a worldwide network of scholars and practitioners.

To learn more about the IIRP Graduate School, go to **www.iirp.edu**.

About the Authors

Bob Costello is Assistant Commissioner for Training and Organizational Development at the New York City Department of Probation and was formerly director of the IIRP's Training and Consulting Division. He has more than 25 years of experience in the fields of mental health, drug and alcohol rehabilitation, inpatient and outpatient services and alternative education. He has brought restorative practices training to professionals across the United States and the world in education, law enforcement and criminal justice, counseling and social work, business and other areas. He has appeared on radio numerous times as a spokesperson for restorative practices and restorative justice, most notably on the acclaimed National Public Radio program, "Justice Talking."

Joshua Wachtel has been a writer for the IIRP since 2006 and earned a Master of Science in Restorative Practices from the IIRP Graduate School in 2015. Joshua lives in western Massachusetts where he works part-time as the IIRP Content Specialist. He has been a teacher since 1995 and employs restorative practices in the workplace and community.

Ted Wachtel is the founder of the International Institute for Restorative Practices, an accredited master's degree-granting graduate school. Wachtel and his wife, Susan, founded the Community Service Foundation and Buxmont Academy (csfbuxmont.org), which operate schools, counseling programs and residential programs in Pennsylvania, employing restorative practices with delinquent and at-risk youth. Wachtel is currently developing projects to expand the field of restorative practices to new areas at BuildingANewReality.com. He has written books, produced videos and conducted keynote presentations and workshops on restorative practices at conferences and events around the world.